The Scottish 4-6-0 Classes

The Scottish 4-6-0 Classes

C. P. Atkins BSc

LONDON
IAN ALLAN LTD

First published 1976

ISBN 0 7110 0700 4

© Ian Allan Ltd.

Published by Ian Allan Ltd, Shepperton, Surrey,
and printed in the United Kingdom by
Ian Allan Printing Ltd.

Dedication

To my wife, Christine

Contents

Preface

Several of the various Scottish 4-6-0 classes have been remarkably little documented in depth in the past which gives refreshing scope to the present-day researcher. They contained a fair proportion of failures which, speaking personally, are every bit as fascinating as the successes for the very reason that they *were* failures. The era in which they flourished is becoming ever more remote and very few, if any, of the men who drove and fired these locomotives are still with us. Fortunately, there are still those who knew these engines in their prime, before their blue and green paint was submerged beneath red and black. In tackling such a subject as the Scottish 4-6-0 it would have been unthinkable not to have consulted Alan Dunbar and David L. Smith, who have answered numerous queries with their much-appreciated customary helpfulness.

Like many others I have long been fascinated by the 'mystery' of the Highland 'River' class. The official record reveals remarkably little and we shall now probably never know the full story with absolute certainty. However, although F. G. Smith himself died nearly twenty years ago, the trail proved to be far from cold. I would like to think I have gone some way in solving the problem. The explanation given here is substantiated by a remark made some years afterwards by Smith's Chief Clerk, Frank Mackenzie who said that 'it was a poor civil engineer who would not allow an extra ton or two.'

In Chapter 9 I have attempted to assess the relative potential of the various Caledonian 4-6-0 classes from published records of their exploits. The use of derived resistance formulae should be treated with the usual caution in the absence of more complete (including prevailing meteorological) data; the figures presented are best used for purposes of comparison, whilst giving some indication of what the engines were and — equally important — were *not* capable of.

The writing of this book would have been quite impossible without the generous assistance of many fellow enthusiasts, too numerous to mention individually, who volunteered personal recollections and anecdotes, and loaned photographs and drawings. However, I would particularly like to thank George Barbour of the Scottish Record Office, William Bulmer and Campbell Highet for much help and encouragement. Thanks are also due to members of the Glasgow & South Western Railway Association for providing details of the two unrealised G&SWR 4-6-0 projects, and to the Editor of the *SLS Journal* for permission to reproduce the diagram of the derived valve gear originally applied to the Caledonian three-cylinder 956 class. Finally I would like to thank Willie Stewart, who prepared the drawings, and my wife for typing the manuscript.   *C. P. A.*

CHAPTER ONE

The 4-6-0 in Scotland

Three of the five major Scottish railway companies which existed prior to 1923, the Highland, the Caledonian and the Glasgow & South Western Railways, made varying use of the 4-6-0 type. As geography and politics would have it these were the same three companies which were, in 1923, to become the Northern Division of the London Midland & Scottish Railway, to which they contributed a total of 1,771 locomotives (1070 CR, 528 G&SWR, and 173 HR). Only 134 of these, or 7½ per cent, were 4-6-0s, but it was a strong measure of the diversity of the contemporary locomotive scene, whose colour was literally about to fade rapidly, that they were made up of no fewer than 16 basic classes. The 4-6-0s were further diversified by several sub-variations, and the actual number of engines in a class varied between only two and nineteen. One Scottish 4-6-0, an accident casualty, was no longer in existence in 1923, but on the credit side twenty new 4-6-0s were built subsequently to a design dating back several years.

The locomotive stock of the former Highland Railway more than made up in quality for its lack of quantity and in the opinion of many, including that of the author, it contributed some of the best locomotives of any of the Scottish railways. One reason was simply because robust outside-cylinder engines predominated, and their boilers were well proportioned in relation to the work to be done. It would hardly be an exaggeration to say that for a crucial period the security of the nation depended upon the tough simplicity of the HR locomotive stock. The existence of a Highland engine was not a glamorous one, but a life of hard slog up severe banks, blasting across desolate windswept landscapes and sometimes battling through winter snows remote from the public eye. Although the type had long been established in the United States the Highland was the British pioneer of the 4-6-0. Compared to the four-coupled engines employed previously it offered greatly superior boiler and adhesive power coupled with only moderate axleloads to tackle the mountain grades.

The original HR 4-6-0 was originally intended to be a freight engine, but in practice proved to be an admirable mixed traffic machine. Developed with a slightly larger boiler and somewhat larger wheels, the resulting 'Castle' remained in intermittent production until as late as 1917. It continued to provide the backbone for secondary passenger services between Perth and Wick for many years subsequently.

Although one of the earliest British users of the 4-6-0 in passenger service, largely on account of severe economic strictures the Highland soon began to lag behind its contemporaries and was slow to catch up with the rapid developments in locomotive engineering of the early 1900s. A man to bring the Highland up to date with a jolt was the unfortunate F. G. Smith. History has not been kind to Smith who, whilst not completely blameless, was not the arrogantly high-handed man some would have us believe. Because he probably failed to consult a fellow officer about the installation of a new turntable, it has often quite wrongly been assumed that he likewise designed and ordered an excessively large 4-6-0 of which the Civil Engineer's department knew nothing until its arrival at Perth. The truth was very different. Smith *had* made a mistake, but only a relatively trivial one, which he was the first to admit; he paid for it with his job. As a result the Highland lost some of the best engines and one of the best engineers in the country at that time.

Succeeding Highland 4-6-0s owed quite a lot to the ill-fated 'Rivers', but lacked some of their more sophisticated refinements, not least their excellent balancing and very low hammerblow. These subsequent Highland 4-6-0s, although popularly ascribed to the name of Cumming, were in fact designed in England on the banks of the River Tyne. It is a curious fact that the precise pedigree of the three earlier HR 4-6-0 classes was also not clearly defined. The working drawings of the 'River' class were uniquely prepared on the drawing boards of quite another railway. The 'Castle', whilst commonly ascribed to Peter Drummond, was merely embellished by him and had originally been envisaged and initiated by David Jones. Delving further back some believe that the direct forerunners of the latter's 'goods' 4-6-0 had already seen service in India and elsewhere before the appearance of these engines between Perth and Inverness.

In contrast to the diverse influences that came to bear upon the evolution of the 4-6-0 on the Highland Railway, the McIntosh 4-6-0s of the Caledonian Railway were thoroughbreds, and as such suffered from the ill-effects of inbreeding. At the turn of the century the reputation of J. F. McIntosh and St Rollox Works rested upon the outstanding exploits of the admirable 'Dunalastair' 4-4-0s, then still in course of development. These epitomised the classic British inside-cylinder 4-4-0, with directly operated slide valves between the cylinders Drummond-style, and a short free-steaming boiler of ample girth having a deep firegrate sunk between the coupled axles. Attempts to extrapolate these fine machines into 4-6-0s were far less successful.

The retention of inside cylinders and therefore a crank axle in such large machines as the big 6ft 6in 4-6-0s was questionable purely on mechanical grounds. One engine did indeed suffer a spectacular failure on its crank axle due to a possible variety of causes. The placing of the cylinder drive on the leading coupled axle also resulted in an inordinately long boiler barrel, to the detriment of free steaming. The boilers of McIntosh's smaller 4-6-0s were not so characterised by excessive length, but compensated for this by having hopelessly inadequate grate areas instead, a deficiency that afflicted *all* the St Rollox 4-6-0 classes to a greater or lesser degree. By the same token the Highland 'River' and 'Clan' designs, and the Manson G&SWR 4-6-0s, would probably have benefited by the provision of slightly larger fireboxes.

McIntosh produced no fewer than six 4-6-0 designs, all with inside cylinders, which numbered only 42 engines in total. These had 5ft, 5ft 9in and 6ft 6in coupled wheels, and were intended for a remarkably wide range of duties; but when judged in the cold light of day only the first and last built could be said to have been genuinely useful and reasonably successful. On the other hand, the big 6ft 6in 4-6-0s were justified and had an immense prestige value, which could not merely be assessed in terms of pounds of tractive effort or tons hauled.

McIntosh's successor, Pickersgill, added three new 4-6-0 classes, which only totalled 18 engines. By virtue of having outside cylinders these eliminated one inherent weakness of the McIntosh 4-6-0s. They were extremely massively built. Pickersgill's 4-6-0s represented little general improvement, however; they displayed the same prodigious appetite for coal, largely on account of their relatively small grates, and were completely lacking in vitality. Construction of the first was already under way when the Caledonian suddenly acquired its best 4-6-0s — the rejected 'Rivers' of the Highland. The latter influenced St Rollox thinking remarkably little, though perhaps they inspired the use of external Walschaerts valve gear in Pickersgill's subsequent 4-6-0 designs and the styling of their footplates.

Pickersgill's balancing techniques were diametrically opposed to those of Smith, as the former's 4-6-0s inflicted savage hammerblow on the permanent way. It is very unlikely that he adopted three-cylinder propulsion in his largest 4-6-0 to reduce track stresses, and probable that he used it simply as a means of obtaining the required cylinder volume in conjunction with a moderate (ie 180lb) boiler working pressure (two equivalent cylinders of 22.7in would have been out of gauge). The result was disastrous: what might have been one of the most outstanding British locomotives to be built before 1923 turned out an abject failure.

One well-known writer of high academic standing made a speciality of describing how a particular locomotive might have been designed differently to better effect, or what might have been produced instead. Pickersgill's best course would have been to take the basic 'River' chassis (suitably reinforced and with 1¼in plates) and place thereon a 200-220lb pressure Belpaire boiler of 5ft 9in maximum girth and 31sq ft grate. Even if the axleload had come out as high as 21tons, this should have been acceptable to a Civil Engineer who had (probably unwittingly) tolerated the ponderous poundings of Pickersgill's two-cylinder 4-6-0s. Such a 'super-River' could have handled the heaviest Caledonian passenger services with distinction.

Pickersgill's last 4-6-0 design was intended as a replacement for the McIntosh 'Oban' 4-6-0s and scarcely reflected 20 years of locomotive engineering progress. By then, towards the end of its days, there were signs that even the Caledonian was becoming disenchanted with the 4-6-0. Latter-day policy was to power its passenger services wherever possible with 4-4-0s. To look after the mixed traffic and heavy freight side a massive 2-6-0 was taking shape on the drawing board.

There was a remarkably similar English parallel in the Great Central Railway, which under J. G. Robinson produced nine classes of 4-6-0 between 1902 and 1921 to cover a wide range of duties. Latterly some of the GCR's best passenger services were operated by a most effective large 4-4-0, the renowned 'Director'

9

class, and Robinson is reputed to have sketched out a 5ft 8in 2-6-0. As was the case on the Caledonian Railway, Robinson's larger 4-6-0s were inhibited by inadequate grate area, which never exceeded 26sq ft (the same as in the 'Director' 4-4-0s). The GC situation was actually even worse, on account of Robinson's primitive ashpan arrangements. The accumulation of ash upon and to the rear of the 'hump' (where the ashpan cleared the trailing coupled axle) could effectively blank off the rear third of the grate towards the end of a run, with the result that steam was being produced by only about half of the ideal grate area. The consumption of coal could be excessively high, a fair proportion passing out of the chimney unburnt.

It is important to remember that McIntosh, Robinson and Pickersgill were all the products of the pre-1914 era when coal was cheap. In 1908 locomotive coal cost the GCR only 9s and the CR 12s per ton. It was said with some truth that one first-class passenger paid the coal bill! McIntosh on his own admission saw greater virtue in locomotive reliability than in fuel economy. There appears to have been great reluctance in many (but by no means *all*) quarters to provide narrow fireboxes with an inside length exceeding about 8ft. Short fireboxes may have been easier to fire in some respects, but the excessive combustion rates they produced must have nearly broken many a fireman! Even if longer grates *had* been provided, it is probable that the corresponding ashpan arrangements would still have been inadequate.

Robinson's larger 4-6-0 boilers were also characterised by the excessive length of their barrels, about 17½ft. McIntosh's 6ft 6in 4-6-0s thus had their English counterparts in the equally striking GCR 'Sir Sam Fay' class, which had even larger (21½in) inside cylinders.

The smaller outside-cylinder mixed-traffic engines were probably Robinson's best 4-6-0 essays, which oddly enough also rather resembled some engines of the Caledonian's bitter rival, the Glasgow & South Western. Although always numerically superior, the G&SWR 4-6-0s in their heyday were overshadowed by McIntosh's blue giants on the rival Glasgow-Carlisle route. In more recent years there has been a tendency to dismiss them as failures, whereas in fact they were mechanically superior, were slightly faster and were certainly more economical on coal. What really mattered, however, was the ability to pull a heavy load and in this respect they certainly were inferior to the St Rollox product.

The 'bad name' of the Manson 4-6-0s probably dates from the immediate post-First World War years, when they were putting up some very mediocre performances simply because they were outdated and badly in need of heavy renewal. By 1920 the employment of saturated steam 4-6-0s elsewhere in Britain on the heaviest main-line passenger services had become quite rare. The GSWR's two superheated 4-6-0s throughout their lives were brilliant performers and could certainly match any Caledonian 4-6-0 (which was not always necessarily saying a great deal). It has mystified many why no more were built. Here again a larger boiler of say, 5ft 6in diameter, 180lb pressure and with 28sq ft of grate would have produced a really capable machine which could possibly have eliminated double-heading. Latterly, as will be described later, it was proposed to fit new larger boilers and cylinders to the saturated engines, but little of the original would have remained.

In 1897 the Glasgow & South Western had built the first British four-cylinder simple locomotive, a decidedly slender-boilered 4-4-0. A larger-boilered version is said to have been rejected in favour of the 4-6-0 five years later and no more four-cylinder engines were ever built at Kilmarnock. However, on the eve of World War I Peter Drummond was preparing drawings for a large four-cylinder 4-6-0, which presents us with one of these fascinating locomotive 'might-have-beens'. Compared to McIntosh's contemporary projected and equally stillborn Caledonian Pacific, it would have been an altogether more realistic proposition. It should have been a good puller, although probably not a very swift machine. Having an exceptionally long and shallow (10ft) grate, the engine's performance could well have been limited by the ability of the fireman to stoke it efficiently, in ironic contrast to what has been said earlier about the Caledonian 4-6-0s.

By the summer of 1903 only the North British Railway of the large Scottish lines was *not* working its prestige passenger services with 4-6-0s. A curious little story that appeared in the *Railway Magazine* for that August was that the General Manager of the NBR had recently permitted the newly formed North British Locomotive Company to carry out 'several exhaustive trials' over its metals with the first of a batch of 32 4-6-0s built to the order of the Canadian Pacific Railway. Whilst presenting a decidedly crude appearance to the refined Edwardian eye, weighing in at 82½tons without tender, the CPR 4-6-0 would have been an ideal engine to cope with the severe gradients of the Waverley Route. It had 20in by 26in cylinders served by inboard piston valves of no less than 12in diameter, 5ft 9in coupled wheels, and an extremely large taper boiler.

It is tempting to suggest that the canny Jackson saw this as a clever way of assessing the potentialities of the 4-6-0 on the NBR without having to borrow one from a neighbouring railway company. Unfortunately it is difficult to see how the engine ever achieved any 'exhaustive trials' over the North British Railway at all, as it measured 15ft 2in to its chimney top, ie it was nearly 2½ft taller than an NB engine and it was almost certainly wider as well. The *Locomotive* (which itself later in January 1908 was to claim that Cowlairs was actually building some 4-6-0s) never reported these alleged trials, although it made frequent reference during the course of 1903 to this unusual export of locomotives from the Old World to the New.

By 1905 the North British Railway was under strong pressure to produce a large new passenger locomotive type in order to try and regain some of its flagging prestige. A contemporary observer could have been forgiven for awaiting the emergence from Cowlairs of a large inside-cylinder 4-6-0, a sort of olive-brown *Cardean*. Dugald Drummond had been in charge at Cowlairs from 1875 to 1882 and had then moved across to St Rollox for eight years. His practices had died hard in both camps and locomotive development on the North British and Caledonian Railways had largely run in parallel until the early 1900s, with the latter generally taking the lead.

Traditionally there was little love lost between the two and quite possibly for this reason Cowlairs came up with something entirely different — an outside-cylinder 4-4-2! The inspiration for the design of this appears to have been the two-cylinder 4-4-2s of the Great Central and North Eastern Railways, each of which had tried *both* the 4-4-2 *and* the 4-6-0 and had come out in favour of the former, of which the principal drawings had been published. The apparent superiority of the 4-4-2 on both the English lines would almost certainly have been due to the ability to provide a deeper firebox and/or a less restricted ashpan layout; it certainly could not be said that the North British 4-4-2s suffered from insufficient firebox capacity. The Cowlairs Atlantic had one of the best-proportioned large boilers of its day.

The reason always given by the NBR for adopting a 4-4-2 in favour of a 4-6-0 was the severe curvature of the Waverley Route, although the line's gradients were equally severe and included 7 miles at a continuous 1 in 75! John Thomas has recently written a very full account of these engines from which it is evident that for quite some time the NBR had considerable misgivings about its 4-4-2s.[*] Originally the more obvious possibility of a 4-6-0 had been quickly dismissed, if it had ever seriously been considered, but after four years when further engines were required it was seriously mooted that these should be built as 4-6-0s (which would have required considerable redesign of the back end). To test this out in October 1910 an NB 4-4-2 made a solitary unrepresentative run between Preston and Carlisle pitted against a smaller LNWR 'Experiment' 4-6-0 and achieved undeserved notoriety in the process. Notwithstanding, further engines were built as 4-4-2s·the following year and two more appeared as late as 1921; these were the last new British Atlantics. One locomotive exchange trial which would have been of exceptional interest would have been to run an NB 4-4-2 over Beattock and a CR 6ft 6in 4-6-0 over the Waverley Route. Ironically both types were tested against the altogether smaller LNWR 'Experiment' 4-6-0, but never against each other. A few myths might thus have been dispelled!

Earlier in 1910 a Highland Railway 'Castle' 4-6-0 had featured in an exchange trial with a North British 'Intermediate' 4-4-0, which on balance came out best. What thinking lay behind this event is not known but two or three years earlier there had been some dissatisfaction with the four-coupled engine when newly introduced on the West Highland line, to the point of prompting consideration of a small-wheeled 4-6-0. This would have resembled the McIntosh 'Oban' 4-6-0, but the curious fact is that this proposal was not made by the NBR's Locomotive Superintendent at all but by its Civil Engineer!

In 1923 the five Scottish main-line railways were swallowed up by either one of two large English-based concerns. A little earlier it had been on the cards that they might be merged into a unified Scottish railway system. Had the latter course been taken, it would have be interesting to speculate which among the inherited types might have become standard. Probably the 4-6-0 would have played a very prominent part in the course of subsequent development. Under British conditions in general a large 4-6-0 was usually adequate to cover most duties. The absence in Scotland of any excessively long non-stop runs would have made the justification for a 4-6-2 with wide firebox difficult. Quite apart

[*]*The North British Atlantics* (David & Charles 1972)

from the additional expense (a very Scottish consideration!), the Pacific when pulling on a heavy grade would have had the additional disadvantage of valuable adhesive weight transferred to the trailing carrying wheels. There would have been some scope for a 4-8-0 if high adhesion and moderate axleload were required, but that could have presented problems in designing a firebox of suitable proportions (either wide or narrow) within the confines of the Scottish loading gauge. It is interesting to note that following the remarkable success of his BR Standard Class 9F 2-10-0, which carried a shallow wide firebox above coupled wheels of relatively small diameter, R. A. Riddles envisaged a very similar stoker-fired 4-8-0 mixed-traffic engine with the Scottish Region of British Railways particularly in mind. Unfortunately time had run out for such new steam development by then, but it would have been an ideal engine for service between Perth and Inverness, the same route for which the first British 4-6-0 had been built just 60 years earlier.

CHAPTER TWO

Locomotives that Won the War

The Highland Railway was the most northerly of the British railway companies. Its single-track main line threaded from Perth up through the Highlands of central Scotland to Inverness, its headquarters, and thence on to Wick, a total distance of 272 miles. Traffic was highly seasonal and could be intensive, with the transport of large quantities of fish, stone and timber at different periods. During the summer months increasing numbers of tourists were carried in rolling stock that was never noted for comfort. The line suffered from the more extreme vagaries of the British climate, often beset by blizzards and blocked by snow in the winter; on occasions during the summer months it was swept away altogether in places by torrential rain.

In the early 1890s the Highland Railway Company was experiencing a moderate prosperity it would never enjoy again; and 20 years later was to assume a strategic importance undreamt of when it came into being in 1865. Prior to 1894 the main-line goods and passenger traffic was in the hands of lightweight outside-cylinder 2-4-0s and 4-4-0s, the only six-coupled engines being a handful of shunting tanks. Then, in February 1894, the Highland very boldly ordered 15 4-6-0 engines of entirely new design at a cost of £2,795 apiece. They were required urgently, for all were delivered between September and mid-November of the same year under penalty. The specification with drawings appeared in *The Engineer* for December 14, 1894, and either by a happy accident or otherwise the same issue contained an extensive feature on the Atlas Works of the builders, Sharp Stewart & Co who had fairly recently removed to Glasgow from Manchester. This feature was accompanied by several 'shop photos' in which the new Highland 4-6-0s prominently appeared in various stages of construction.

Over the years there has been some debate as to the precise origins of the design of this, the first British 4-6-0, and as to its supposed derivation from a certain prolific Indian locomotive class. Suffice it to say that the credit for its adoption and success should fall squarely on the shoulders of David Jones, the HR Locomotive Superintendent. It says much for his original concept that, disregarding inevitable and purely superficial modifications, the engines remained basically unaltered throughout their long and useful lives. These extended well into a regime pursuing a policy of ruthless locomotive standardisation, which brought about the early demise of many more recent and more numerous examples of the same wheel arrangement from other lines.

The Highland had thus, for the moment, obviated the 0-6-0 employed by practically every other British railway except the HR's neighbour and bitter enemy, the Great North of Scotland. A 0-6-0, however, would have meant a crank axle, and crank axles did not have a place in Jones' book. Jones was a fervent disciple of Alexander Allan, but one Allan feature Jones did not perpetuate in his 4-6-0s was double framing around the outside cylinders. Allan's straight link valve gear was retained; this was basically similar to the corresponding Stephenson gear, but the link was easier and therefore cheaper to make and imparted a constant lead irrespective of cut-off.

A unique trademark of Jones' locomotives was a louvred chimney. Its precise intended function is a mystery. The *Engineer* article stated that it was 'held to augment the draught', but as the louvres admitted only to the open annular space between the inner and outer chimneys this defies elementary physics. The same journal for July 8, 1898, in respect of the Jones 'Loch' 4-4-0, claimed that the chimneys were 'fitted with a device for inducing an air draught which also tends to prevent the distribution of sparks.' It would therefore appear that these chimneys were genuinely believed to assist steaming without resort to means that would have increased cylinder back pressure, which would certainly have been caused by installation of an internal smokebox spark arrester. Every year the company was obliged to pay out compensation for lineside fires started by its locomotives, but a possible reduction in spark throwing would seem to have been only a minor and uncovenanted benefit of fitting these chimneys.

Excepting the Mersey Railway 0-6-4Ts of 1885-6, whose duties were in any case of an intermittent nature, the Jones 4-6-0 had the largest cylinders of any British locomotive yet built, and furthermore the boiler capacity to match. Although built on to substantial plate frames 1¼in thick, the 4-6-0's axleload did not exceed 14½tons. As a result the adhesive factor was decidedly low at 3.8 on an engine required to haul up to 45 loaded wagons up 7¾ miles of 1 in 70 approaching the 1485ft. summit at Drumochter, and on an often greasy rail. One old driver has recalled that, when he was working on the engines on fish trains in later years and the passage of several similar earlier trains had covered the rails in slime, it was not always readily possible in darkness to know whether any forward progress was being made at all!

Notwithstanding, the Jones 4-6-0s Nos 103 to 117 were all dearly loved by the men. All started life in identical form except that Nos 106 and 116 had the Westinghouse brake in order to work 'foreign' stock coming off the Caledonian and North British at Perth. When new, the Jones 4-6-0s were frequently pressed into passenger service in the summer season. When only a few weeks old one attained 60mph for several miles downhill and the class was allowed 200 tons unaided over much of the Perth-Inverness main line, except for assistance over the summits at Drumochter and Dava.

Seemingly Jones' last locomotive design was a 4-4-0, the 'Loch', of which 15 were delivered by Dübs in 1896. Built very much in the same mould as the goods 4-6-0s, these ranked amongst the largest British passenger engines of the day, but were limited to a load of 120 tons. However, by the time they appeared the eminent success of the goods 4-6-0s prompted design of a larger-wheeled and slightly larger-boilered passenger version. Unfortunately Jones was obliged to retire prematurely in October 1896 as a direct result of scalds inflicted on his legs two years earlier by an injector overflow when he was personally testing the first of the goods 4-6-0s newly received from the makers.

Jones was succeeded at Lochgorm by Peter Drummond, younger brother of the formidable Dugald. Possibly for economy reasons the passenger 4-6-0 proposal was shelved, but in the summer of 1899 the heavy summer tourist traffic for the first time passed over the new Direct Route via Carr Bridge that had been opened a few months earlier. Whilst the new line substantially reduced the distance between Perth and Inverness from 144 to 118 miles, and the best travelling time by ¾ hour to 3¼ hours, both approaches to its 1315ft summit at Slochd involved gradients of 1 in 60. Here the Jones 4-6-0s really showed up to advantage, which must have prompted hasty dusting down of the drawings for the projected passenger 4-6-0, as six such engines were delivered by Dübs in June 1900 just in time for the next summer season.

Whereas the Jones 4-6-0s — generally referred to as the 'Big Goods' — had been designed, built and put into traffic all within a single year, the 'Castles', as they came to be known, were in gestation for nearly four years. By the time they did appear the North Eastern Railway had built the first British passenger 4-6-0 a year earlier. On to the stylish lines of David Jones was grafted the heavy finish of Peter Drummond. Although mechanically the new engines were pure Jones, their Drummond stamp of chimney, cab and ugly 'water-cart' bogie tender was unmistakable. A dubious asset, without which none of the younger Drummond's locomotives was complete, was the provision of steam reverse, a troublesome mechanism if it were not well maintained.

According to a contemporary account, the first six 'Castles' were all stationed at Perth, whence they each made five round trips per week to Inverness. Four more, Westinghouse-fitted, came from the same builders in 1902, and were likewise adorned in an ornate lined green livery. But at the turn of the century the Highland company was in desperate financial straits. In the interests of strict economy passenger locomotives were turned out in a plain green livery from the start of 1903.

The cash position had improved little six years later when two more 'Castles' were ordered from what was now the North British Locomotive Company, as the Highland stipulated that delivery was to be made one engine at a time a year apart. When the second of these was despatched from Queens Park Works in March 1911 the shops were in the curious position of working round the clock on an order for 30 engines to the same drawings (20 more were concurrently under construction at the NBL's Hyde Park Works) for service in France! Desperate for new motive power and deciding that the Highland 'Castle' suited its requirements, the French State Railways had ordered 50 such engines from NBL in January 1911 on condition that all would be fully erected and on the rails in France by the end of the following June. This requirement was satisfactorily met and the engines, modified only in minor details, ran in secondary service until withdrawn between 1933 and 1937. Many were cut up on quaysides in Northern France just prior to the war, and the forlorn fate of three such engines was illustrated in the *Railway Magazine* for January 1941.

Locomotive interchange trials were all the rage at this time. Early in 1910 No 146 *Skibo Castle* ran competitive trials against North British 'Intermediate' 4-4-0 No 867 between Blair Atholl and Dalwhinnie on the HR, and between Perth and Kinross on the NBR. It was reported that the four-coupled engine came off best on both occasions and presumably scotched any thoughts of a possible NBR 4-6-0.

A good account by B. Purvis of the everyday work of the 'Castles' in their heyday appeared in the *Railway Magazine* for March 1913. A run was quoted behind No 149 *Duncraig Castle* heading 175 tons unassisted on the 3.50pm ex-Inverness. Slochd Summit was reached in 44min 35sec, entailing a vertical climb of 1286ft in 23 miles. In the reverse direction the 11.50am ex-Perth was scheduled to make its first stop at Newtonmore, 68¾ miles, in 114min, which was the longest non-stop run on the system for many years. This included a 1454ft rise to Drumochter Summit, over which trains were frequently assisted by a 'Loch' 4-4-0 as pilot. Limited to 200 tons without a pilot, the 'Castles' could maintain 25mph up the most severe 1 in 60 gradients approaching Slochd either northbound or southbound. Factor of adhesion was around 4.5 and gravity sanding was applied to the front of the flangeless centre coupled wheels only. Most schedules required average running speeds of about 40mph and mile-a-minute descents of the banks were common. A 'Castle' could be pushed under protest to about 70mph downhill. Its cylinders and straight link valve gear were very similar to those of the Jones 4-6-0s. Probably the original intention was to give the 'Castles' piston valves, but the remarkable non-success of these in the 'Loch' 4-4-0s as originally built prompted the adoption of Richardson balanced slide valves in these passenger 4-6-0s.

Even by 1913 the day of the 'Castle' was by no means done. More were on order and early the previous year No 141 *Ballindalloch Castle* was experimentally equipped with a Phoenix smokebox superheater at the expense of the proprietors. This consisted of a nest of steampipes in an extended smokebox, upon the leading end of which the chimney was absurdly placed. Evaluation of the device, which was also tried by several other British railways about that time, was delayed by the 1912 Coal Strike, but it was soon abundantly apparent that it had no practical value and it was removed after a very short time, although the longer smokebox lasted until about 1917.

This diversion was made without doubt at the instigation of Drummond's Works Manager, F.G. Smith, who delighted in gadgetry and who succeeded him as Locomotive Superintendent at Lochgorm in February 1912. The engine concerned was the regular charge of Will Tulloch, who had in the past worked the Royal Train with it. Tulloch was the star driver at Perth shed and was highly regarded by at least three successive locomotive superintendents. Smith later earmarked him to test drive *River Ness*, but, presumably denied that interesting task, he later participated in trials with the oil-burning 4-6-0 *Clan Stewart* in 1921.

Smith visited NBL in August 1912 to discuss modifications in further 'Castles', a firm order for four of which followed a few days later at an agreed cost of £4190 each. The earlier 'Castles' had a rather 'flat-chested' look and the appearance of the new engines was to be considerably improved by extended smokeboxes topped by slightly taller chimneys. There were numerous other refinements, including modified fireboxes with improved staying and thicker foundation rings, and the adoption of solid big ends in place of the clumsy Drummond marine type. These engines arrived during 1913, when attempts were made to secure tenders for another four 'Castles', but British locomotive builders were very heavily booked at the time and there were no offers.

There is no truth in the suggestion that a 'Castle' was equipped with either a Schmidt or a Smith superheater. There were proposals to fit an engine of this type with Smith's own pattern of feedwater heater, but they do not appear to have matured.

Preparations had recently been made to use the 'Castles' north of Inverness. On May 23, 1913 No 143 *Gordon Castle* broke new ground by hauling a special twelve-coach train, aggregating 260 tons and conveying Highland directors and officials, to Wick, from whence it returned the next day. It was the announced intention to use the 'Castles', then newly delivered, north of Inverness, but in fact it fell to two of the oldest members of the class, Nos 140 and 145, to work the North Mails in the remaining months of peace.

Eventual war with Germany had long been anticipated. The outcome would largely hinge on the balance of naval power in the North Sea. The Grand Fleet immediately came into being and was despatched with the utmost secrecy to the desolate Orkney anchorage of Scapa Flow.

Overnight, without any prior warning whatever, the Highland Railway was called upon to carry an immense extra traffic in men, munitions and supplies. The warships were all coal-fired, but mercifully most of the coal hauled up by rail from South Wales in the famed 'Jellicoe Specials' went by sea from Grangemouth to Scapa. However, domestic coal which formerly was largely sent by sea now went north by rail, sometimes double-headed by Jones 4-6-0s, so that these engines were now seen north of Inverness on occasion.

Some idea of the strain put on HR resources may be gauged from these statistics:

Year	Passengers carried	Freight tonnage
1913	2,222,703	653,589
1914	2,292,435	771,454
1915	3,477,787	928,874
1916	4,516,277	1,134,615
1917	3,779,659	1,305,659
1918	3,344,480	1,323,437

At the Annual Shareholders' Meeting in March 1916 the Chairman remarked that 'We have carried traffic which would have overtaxed a double line throughout from Perth to Wick and Thurso ... Frankly I think the fact that we have not "stuck" can only be ascribed to something like a miracle.'

The Jones 4-6-0s had quite fortuitously been braced for the unexpected task ahead, for all had been reboilered between 1910 and 1913. However after the war had been in progress for one year the Highland Railway was at breaking point. Out of a total locomotive stock of 152, 50 engines were laid up awaiting repairs and another 50 were badly in need of them. To exacerbate the situation most of the regular fitters at Lochgorm had joined the armed services immediately war was declared, contrary to Government instructions.

A special meeting of the Railway Executive Committee was convened at Perth on September 7, 1915 at which F.G. Smith, Locomotive Superintendent, Alexander Newlands, Chief Engineer, and William Whitelaw, Deputy Chairman, met locomotive officers from several other leading railways in order to try and secure the loan of some locomotives. Help was not very forthcoming and what was received could only be described in some cases as very elderly 'castoffs'. However, even had they been available many modern engines would have been too heavy for HR metals and anything on wheels that would steam was desperately needed. Two years later, faced with the prospect of having to give up even these doubtful assets for service overseas, the Highland felt obliged to inform the REC that in such an event it would 'decline all responsibility for transport of Government material and men in the North.'

Unfortunately the Memorandum of the Perth meeting no longer survives, but according to p.36 of the SLS publication on the Highland Railway the Company stated that the 'best use was not made of monies granted for locomotive repairs in the few years before the War.' Reading between the lines, one suspects that Smith could already have been under a cloud before the arrival a few days later of the first of the long-awaited superheater 4-6-0s, whose rejection by the Chief Engineer directly led to Smith's resignation at the end of the month.

In the vacuum thus created Whitelaw temporarily took charge of locomotive affairs and contracted with NBL to build three 'Loch' 4-4-0s, complete with louvred chimneys, plus three more 'Castles'. The latter were based on the 1913 batch, but for some reason, which can only have delayed delivery, the driving wheels were increased to 6ft diameter and new pattern six-wheeled tenders were to be attached. More sensibly the specification of screw reverse must have reflected the difficulties being experienced with the standard steam reverse under adverse maintenance conditions. Delivery, originally promised in 8 months by the builders, was greatly delayed by the pressure of other wartime work. Costing £5,425 each the three engines were eventually delivered at the end of March and the beginning of April 1917, but evidently they did not give every satisfaction. The HR Locomotive Committee Minutes for May 9, 1917 cryptically record that 'Mr Cumming reported on the new Castle Engines and it was agreed to write North British Locomotive Company regarding their condition.' Unfortunately just what was wrong with the engines is not revealed but it is subsequently recorded that Cumming had visited NBL and 'made arrangements' regarding them. The trials and tribulations of the Highland Railway during World War I could alone warrant a book of this size in their own right.

Meanwhile, arrangements were made to repair some of the existing locomotive stock outside. At least one Jones 4-6-0 was repaired at Cowlairs, NBR, whilst five came south of the Border for repair in England. During 1916, 109 and 115 were overhauled by the Yorkshire Engine Co in Sheffield, 103 by Robert Stephenson & Co in Darlington, 107 in Newcastle by Hawthorn Leslie & Co, and 112 was repaired just across the river at Gateshead Works, NER.

After the war had ended two of these came south again when 103 and 112 were repaired by Hawthorn Leslie during 1920-21 along with 'Castles' 28 and 143. By this time the goods 4-6-0s were of somewhat variable appearance. Some engines had lost their smokebox wingplates quite early and in many such cases Drummond type chimneys later quite altered their appearance in LMS days. One or two engines sported a louvred chimney with a Drummond top!

For their part the 'Castles' must have featured prominently in the working of the heavy fourteen-coach Naval Specials instituted in February 1917. The northbound train was always known as 'the Misery', taking sailors back to the northern bases from leave in the south. The total 717mile journey from Euston to Thurso was scheduled to take 21½hours, just over 10 of which were occupied in traversing Highland metals north of Perth. Heavy track occupation and periodic locomotive failures must sometimes have prolonged this wearisome journey still further, making even the prospect of a berth in a battleship a delightful one!

By the time the final 1917 trio appeared the older 'Castles' were falling due for heavy renewal and during 1916-7 six new boilers were ordered from Kitson & Co and Robert Stephenson & Co. Most engines eventually received new boilers, a process which continued well into LMS days. Two of the 1900 engines, *Blair Castle* and *Murthly Castle,* were rebuilt in 1926 with new, slightly modified boilers having extended smokeboxes. The latter engine was the first 'Castle' to be scrapped four years later and its boiler passed to *Gordon Castle.* About this time *Brahan Castle* acquired a Derby-pattern smokebox door, and *Beaufort Castle* sported an unusually short chimney, both probably because of a shortage of the correct spare parts.

In LMS days the 'Castles' could be encountered anywhere between Perth and Wick. Hitherto confined to Perth and Inverness sheds, odd examples were stabled at Aviemore, Forres, Helmsdale and Wick. After years of unceasing north-south hard slog, a few in 1936 appeared on the Oban line, sometimes working through between Oban and Dundee. *Skibo Castle* and *Urquhart Castle* were shedded at Balornock and acquired six-wheeled tenders off two of the 1917-built engines. The war reprieved several of the 'Castles' and a representative of each delivery was still in existence as late as 1945. The last survivor, at Aviemore, was *Dalcross Castle,* condemned in April 1947, having covered 925,290 miles with its original boiler; it was cut up at Lochgorm a few weeks before nationalisation.

The Jones 4-6-0s also soldiered on well after 1923 and one or two ended their days on the line to Kyle of Lochalsh. The final example did not disappear until a few months after the outbreak of the Second World War, and the last survivors were much in evidence during their final months.

The pioneer No 103 was retired in July 1934 but was thoughtfully restored by the LMSR at St Rollox to the elaborate lined pea-green HR livery of the 1890s. A genuine louvred chimney was refitted, but the smokebox wingplates were not at this stage restored. In this condition the engine can rarely have been seen by the general public, but the situation was remedied after no less than 25 years of inactivity. In 1959 what was now the Scottish Region of British Railways restored the engine to full working order to haul enthusiasts' special trains. In the course of its second restoration wingplates were provided and No 103 was completely repainted in a striking Stroudleyesque yellow livery. This was apparently carried out in the genuine belief that the engine had actually been turned out in such a livery when brand new, although it was quickly repainted in the standard pea green paint.

Many a railway historian must wish that commercial colour photography had been available a few decades earlier to settle disputed points concerning erstwhile locomotive liveries. However, there is little strong evidence to suggest that the first two or three Jones 4-6-0s were delivered painted yellow, but it is no doubt in this style that the engine will be admired for many years to come.

After seven years of special excursion work, during which No 103 came south of the Border and briefly featured in a popular film, the engine was retired to Glasgow Museum of Transport in 1966. However, in view of the fact that in the past a number of preserved locomotives, including No 103 itself, have successfully been returned to active service after many years out of steam and the fact that this engine was at work until comparatively recently, it is not outside the bounds of possibility that at some stage in the future No 103 might once again head north from Perth.

Jones 4-6-0s (all engines reboilered during 1910-1913)

HR Nos	Builder	Works Nos	Date	LMS Nos	Withdrawn
103-117	Sharp Stewart	4022-4036	1894	17916-17930	1929-1940

Castle Class* (most engines reboilered between 1917 and 1930)

HR Nos	Builder	Works Nos	Date	LMS Nos	Withdrawn
140-145	Dübs	3848-3853	1900	14675-14680	1930-1946
146-149	Dübs	4244-4247	1902	14681-14684	1937-1946
30, 35	NBL	19011, 19012	1910, 1911	14685, 14686	1945, 1946
26-29†	NBL	20160-20163	1913	14687-14690	1935-1947
50, 58, 59	NBL	21459-21461	1917	14691-14693	1935-1946

* For names see Chapter 12.

† No 29 was delivered as HR No 43, but almost immediately exchanged numbers with Drummond 0-6-4T No 29.

CHAPTER THREE

F. G. Smith and the 'Rivers'

The six F. G. Smith 4-6-0s of 1915 have a unique place in British locomotive history. To this day generally referred to as the 'Highland Rivers', only two of the six ever briefly sported Highland green livery and were named, and yet no *authentic* photograph of either of them in this condition is known to exist. In addition, what little has been written about their unfortunate and talented designer has had, in the main, scarcely any basis on actual fact. Even his full name has frequently been misquoted.

The first hint that the average railway enthusiast would have had about these engines was to be found in the April issue of *The Locomotive*. 'The new 4-6-0 express engines which Messrs Hawthorn Leslie & Co Ltd are building are larger than any engines so far in service on the Highland line', it announced. 'Six of these engines, Nos 70 to 75, will be delivered in June... They will have Belpaire fireboxes, and the Ross pop safety valve, and will be provided with the patent water heating arrangements invented by Mr F. G. Smith, Chief Mechanical Engineer of the H.Ry. who, of course, has prepared the designs of these engines.'

A few months later in its November issue the same journal remarked that 'two of the new express engines, No 70 *River Ness* and No 71 *River Spey,* were delivered by the makers recently, but we understand these have now been sold to the Caledonian Ry.' On another page was a brief reference to the effect that Smith had resigned and that a successor had been appointed.

Frederick George Smith was born in Newcastle-upon-Tyne at 15 East Parade on April 20, 1872. He was no relation of W. M. ('Compound') Smith. His father had recently moved from Hull as a District Passenger Superintendent on the North Eastern Railway and much of Smith's childhood was spent at Picton House, formerly the terminus of the Blyth & Tyne Railway. He was educated at a good day school in Newcastle run by a Dr Erlich, and in 1888 he commenced a five-year apprenticeship under Thomas Worsdell at Gateshead Works, NER. On completion of this Smith spent a further seven years in the employ of the NER, including some time at Gateshead, Middlesbrough, Shildon and Blaydon running sheds. He had a spell in the Westinghouse Brake Department, and in this capacity enjoyed one brief moment of glory during the 1895 Race to the North when he frantically and successfully replaced a defective pipe on a locomotive whilst it was taking water at Newcastle.

At the turn of the century Smith decided to broaden his outlook and left the North Eastern to become CME to G. F. Milnes & Co, the tramcar builders at Hadley Castle, which he soon left to become a partner in the Crown Iron Foundry in Birmingham. This too soon proved unsatisfactory and evidently more to his liking was the post of Chief Mechanical Inspector to Crompton & Co of Chelmsford, the electrical engineers. Smith remained in Essex for three years and during this time devised and made for himself an electric blanket long before such comforts became available commercially.

Smith had a most inventive turn of mind and was years ahead of his time in several spheres. An early motorist, he originally drove a White steam car, but upon graduation to internal combustion his vehicles did not escape his ingenuity. He fitted an auxiliary gearbox to one which amounted to an overdrive and also effected considerable fuel economy by inserting a variable air inlet, controlled from the dashboard, between the carburettor and inlet manifold. When fully opened this also enabled the engine to be used as a brake. Another car he modified to run on naphtha instead of petrol once the engine had warmed up; at that time costing eightpence a gallon naphtha was later made illegal as a motor fuel.

It was Smith's outside experience of industry, compared to that of the other applicants, that secured him the post of Works Manager to the Highland Railway at Inverness at the end of 1903. Here he improved workshop procedures by instituting something akin to 'production line' methods. He appears to have enjoyed a satisfactory relationship with Peter Drummond, whom he succeeded as Locomotive, Carriage and Wagon Superintendent in February 1912.

A smart, very erect man, Smith carried himself with military bearing, a lifelong trait no doubt resulting from his service with the Royal Engineers Volunteers in the 1890s, which he had left with the rank of Captain upon departing from Newcastle. Endowed with a somewhat inflexible temperament, he nevertheless displayed a genial disposition and a brisk sense of humour, and spoke with no trace of a Geordie accent. He contrasted strongly with his unpopular and rather unimaginative predecessor.

Drummond's locomotives displayed a healthy appetite for coal and Smith patented a feedwater heater utilising the waste heat in the smokebox gases and exhaust steam. In its limited and short-lived applications, mainly to Drummond 'Large Ben' 4-4-0s and a 0-6-4T, this effected appreciable fuel economy but proved troublesome to maintain.

If by 1913 it was becoming necessary to use 'Castles' north of Inverness, then the introduction of something larger and more powerful on the Perth road was long overdue. Smith drew up specifications for a modern superheated 4-6-0, but at this time the Locomotive Department only employed a single draughtsman and so detailed drawings had to be prepared elsewhere. Arrangements were made through William Whitelaw, who was currently both Deputy Chairman of the Highland, and Chairman of the North British railways, to have drawings made at Cowlairs Drawing Office at a maximum cost of £200. A curious aspect of this possibly unique transaction is that the official record refers to the engines as 'Castles'; the decision to name the engines after Scottish rivers was not made until 14 months later at the end of March 1915.

Following the outbreak of war and the Highland's new found strategic importance, tenders were invited for the construction of six of the new engines. On September 29, 1914 the Board resolved to award the contract to Hawthorn

Leslie & Co of Newcastle-upon-Tyne, on the understanding that the engines would be delivered in pairs during May, June and July 1915 at a cost of £4,920 each.

The choice of builder was a curious one, but one which probably had nothing to do with Smith's Tyneside origins. A long-established firm, Hawthorn Leslie & Co, had only recently started building large main-line locomotives for the home market with ten 0-6-4Ts for the Barry Railway in 1914. Predictably the Highland's usual supplier, NBL, had put in a tender for the contract, but like the other more traditional builders would still have been heavily booked with other orders and Hawthorn Leslie probably offered the shortest delivery time. Their works occupied a very restricted site above the River Tyne at Forth Bank incorporating a part of Robert Stephenson's original works, immediately beneath Newcastle Central Station. New locomotives had to be propelled up a very steep incline to gain access to the North Eastern Railway metals above.

Actual delivery was nevertheless delayed and by the time the first engine arrived at Perth in September the Highland Railway was in really desperate straits, as related in the previous chapter. The crisis was further exacerbated by the refusal of Newlands, the Chief Engineer, to allow the use of the new 4-6-0.

Much has been made of the emnity alleged to have existed between Newlands and Smith, but this was probably no more than a simple clash of personalities between two strong and intransigent heads of department with sometimes conflicting interests. By all accounts Newlands could be a difficult man, and Smith a stubborn one. Earlier there had been friction over the new turntable at Inverness.

In November 1913 Smith had ordered from Cowans Sheldon Ltd a 60ft replacement for the old 55ft turntable at Inverness. Whilst the turntable itself *was* Smith's responsibility, its pit was the concern of the Chief Engineer. Almost immediately upon his promotion from Assistant to Chief Engineer in January 1914, in succession to William Roberts, Newlands had raised objections to making the modifications which would be required. The only satisfactory solution had been to cancel the order and replace it by an even larger non-standard 63ft 2in table, which was delivered at the end of April 1914.

The original turntable was ordered when William Roberts was still Chief Engineer, though whether he had been consulted in this matter we do not know. It must have been about this time also that Smith began to plan his new 4-6-0. Contrary to popular myth this must have been referred to the Chief Engineer's department, because Newlands' objection to the engine, of which he was fully aware, upon its arrival was that it exceeded its estimated weight.

It was by no means unusual for a new locomotive type to exceed its estimated weight, the first Pacifics of Stanier and Bulleid are both said to have exceeded the estimate by several tons. Smith told his nephew that his draughtsman had omitted to allow for the superheater when originally estimating the total weight, a factor which he had also overlooked when later checking the figures. This would have resulted in an underestimate of only one or two tons. In the case of contractor-built locomotives of new design, it was normal practice to allow 2½ per cent on either side of the estimated weight as calculated by the builder when submitting his tender.

By nature a meticulous and methodical man, Smith insisted as head of his department on taking full responsibility for the oversight when questioned by the directors at the Special Board Meeting hurriedly convened at Perth to discuss the impasse on September 24. Newlands was not present but his department had calculated the stresses the new 4-6-0 would impose on structures out on the main line. A contemporary reference to Newlands' promotion to Chief Engineer observed that previously he had 'supervised the renewal of many of the viaducts and bridges on the Highland Railway system'. It is to be presumed that his interpretation of what loads these could now bear was more conservative than that of his predecessor Roberts. Later events were to prove that he had indeed been unnecessarily restrictive. A pedantic man, Newlands could well have seized upon the excess weight of the new engine in order to make an issue of its total weight which he personally regarded as extravagant. It is believed that the structures deemed to be at risk were of a relatively minor nature, and were little more than culverts.

Several years later Smith's former Chief Clerk, Frank Mackenzie, remarked that 'it was a poor civil engineer who would not accept an extra ton or two'. However, the often quoted official record reads that the new engine was 'now found to be considerably heavier than the Directors had anticipated'. When questioned by a shareholder some months later the Chairman replied that the engine had 'proved when delivered to be too heavy in axle-weight within the limited length of wheelbase'. The axleload itself was below the 17.8 tons of the Drummond 'Large Ben' 4-4-0s of 1908, but evidently the weight per foot run gave rise to concern. (In 1919 two ROD 2-8-0s, which were heavier still in this respect, were actually earmarked for the HR but never used thereon.) There is no reference to the engine being out of gauge as has sometimes been suggested. The HR loading gauge was unusually generous and would only have been ever fully exploited in the 'River' design as originally built. The maximum height of 13ft 3¾in was also attained by the seven 'Castle' 4-6-0s built in 1913-17, whilst the maximum width over cylinders of 8ft 10½in was equalled in subsequent new engines built for the line to the order of Smith's successor.

On this account it is therefore by no means impossible that *River Ness* at least reached Inverness for general inspection purposes, but whether it did actually get north of Perth is shrouded in mystery. Writing in the *SLS Journal* for June 1969, Graham Langmuir related that as a child standing in Pitlochry station in 1915 he had pointed out to him 'a big engine going to Inverness which was larger than anything on the line and quite unlike them.' The date is given as Glasgow Fairs Friday (July 23), which rather rules out the possibility that it had been *River Ness* as he later thought, although on the other hand it is very difficult to suggest what it was that he did see. A correspondent categorically claims to have witnessed the second engine, *River Spey,* in Highland green (lined out in red) on Aviemore shed. This alleged sighting is in line with the popular tradition that the first two 'Rivers' were delivered to the Highland. The Company Minutes, however, only refer to one. This in turn is supported by the personal recollection of Mr Arthur Gill, a former draughtsman at Forth Banks, that only *River Ness* was actually delivered in plain green paint and lettered 'H.R'.

River Spey was also similarly finished by the builders, but repainted *dark* blue by them prior to despatch to the Caledonian Railway, who bought the six engines following the refusal of the Highland to accept them.

At the Board meeting on September 24 Smith had been asked to tender his immediate resignation on account of the engines. The possibility cannot be discounted, however, that he was also removed for political reasons, ie the desperate situation regarding the entire Highland locomotive fleet at that time. Smith bore no malice and rarely if ever referred to the matter again. His wife Lilian, however, would bitterly remark that if he had had a 'Mac' in front of his name 'all would have been well'. A woman of strong character, she personally held Newlands responsible for what had happened. Smith returned to his native North-East, where he almost immediately secured a post as an Assistant to the Comptroller of the Ministry of Munitions. This consisted of supervising and allocating contracts for the manufacture of wooden shell boxes in the North of England. His chief was David Bain, the eminent carriage designer, a Scot and himself an ex-Gateshead man. Bain successfully proposed Smith for Membership of the Institution of Mechanical Engineers in June 1918.

No full description of the 'River' 4-6-0 ever appeared in the technical press. Without a doubt they were the most advanced 4-6-0s to be built for any British railway other than the Great Western prior to 1923. Their inspiration had been the R.W. Urie 6ft mixed-traffic H15 class 4-6-0 of the London & South Western Railway, of which the first, No 486, had been completed at Eastleigh at the end of 1913. On encountering Urie at a Euston meeting shortly afterwards Smith had professed his admiration for the former's new engine and stated his intention to build something similar for the Highland Railway. Whilst utilising the same cylinder dimensions and coupled wheel diameter, of necessity the Smith engine was a lighter machine and incorporated a smaller Belpaire boiler. It is interesting to note that Urie and Smith had both functioned as works managers under the two Drummond brothers. Upon succeeding the latter in office (both in 1912) each had perpetuated the characteristic, robust Drummond style of construction, but with the immediate adoption of two outside cylinders and the superheater. Labour-saving devices, particularly of a domestic nature, were a lifelong preoccupation with Smith and in the 'Rivers' he introduced a robust short-lap, short-travel Walschaerts valve gear ($1in/4\frac{7}{8}in$) fully exposed outside the frames for the first time in a Scottish locomotive, in conjunction with 10in diameter piston valves. To assist servicing further a drop grate was provided, and Smith's own design of feedwater heater was concealed within the smokebox and between the frames. The Belpaire boiler was designed to work at 180lb pressure, but in actual service pressure never exceeded 160lb, regulated by Ross 'pop' safety valves, their first application in Scotland. The Schmidt superheater had originally been specified, but possibly for patriotic reasons the Robin son pattern was actually employed, although on practical grounds the North British and Caledonian concerns had both come to prefer the English apparatus by 1915. The large tenders were the heaviest on six wheels so far built for a British railway, and certainly would not have eased any weight problems.

To the casual observer about the only discernible hallmark of Cowlairs would have been the inverted crescent handrail on the smokebox door. However, a number of components, eg the slidebars, crosshead, and drop grate, were very closely modelled on those of the North British 4-4-2s, the nearest thing Cowlairs had produced for home consumption. The original design of chimney is only illustrated in the maker's official photographs. One of these shows an engine, fully lined out, devoid of number, name or legend. Another identical view shows the same engine numbered 70, named *River Ness* and lettered 'Highland Railway' in full on the tender. In fact the maker's plate indentifies the engine as being the *last* of the six, *alias* CR 943, whose picture as such was also evidently taken at the same sitting, as the engine (not to say to camera) has not moved although a shorter chimney has been substituted and the tender coal plates have been removed!

As mentioned earlier the 'Rivers' were sold to the Caledonian, who paid £5400 each for them, thereby somehow netting the Highland a total profit of £2880 on several engines it had not even taken delivery of. St Rollox required a number of modifications to be made at a total cost of £140. *River Ness* did not return to the builders, but it and the briefly named *River Spey* were subsequently distinguished by handsome built-up chimneys with capuchons, which were probably the originals shortened to give a maximum height of 13ft 0in. The remaining engines were given less pleasing Pickersgill-style flared chimneys 2in shorter still. Also to conform with the Caledonian loading gauge the tender coal plates were removed. The builder's general arrangement drawing for these last four engines shows the Smith feedwater heater still *in situ,* but this is said to have been taken out prior to delivery thus reducing the weight by half a ton. (The drop grates were also soon removed.) The CR and LMS always quoted the maximum axleload as being 17¾ tons, whereas the HR Engineers Office diagram dated September 15, 1915, on which the latter's objections were no doubt based, gave this as only 17⅓ tons! This diagram indicates that the centre driving wheel tyres were to have been flangeless as in the Jones 4-6-0s and 'Castles'; as supplied to the Caledonian the wheels all were fully flanged.

When new, the last two engines, as CR Nos 942 and 943, were stationed at Perth and for about a year put up some very fine but apparently undocumented performances between Glasgow Buchanan Street and Perth. They are said to have gained handsomely on schedules and put the thoroughbred St Rollox 4-6-0s in the shade to the point of embarrassment. They soon found themselves on fast goods workings at Carlisle, which they shared with the other four engines that were based on Balornock. They only criticism of these engines was their troublesome steam reverse, which proved difficult to maintain. By later CR days the original sombre Hawthorn Leslie dark blue livery had disappeared beneath the sparkling sky blue of St Rollox.

Under LMS auspices the design could have formed a standard mixed traffic class capable of running over the main lines of all three major constituents of the Northern Division of the LMSR. An equivalent number would have been a much better investment than the 20 Pickersgill '60' class 4-6-0s turned out of St Rollox during 1925-26. Only their short travel valves and 'Z' steam ports, and possibly excessive width over cylinders, could have stood against them being adopted as a system-wide standard class had anyone been enlightened enough even to consider them. Had they been re-designed in a similar manner to that applied on the Southern Railway by R. E. L. Maunsell to the Urie N15 4-6-0s the Stanier Class 5 might never have been built.

An ironic twist to the 'River Affair' came in the summer of 1928 when the engines began to operate regularly between Perth and Inverness! Opinion is divided as to whether bridge strengthening of any consequence had been carried out to permit this; a photograph exists of the two Perth 'Rivers' and an ex-CR three-cylinder 4-6-0 all in pre-1928 LMS livery and in tandem coming off the Tay Bridge at Dalguise. The circumstances of this occurrence are uncertain, but in December 1928 the Bridge Stress Committee published its findings. Over the course of five years the Committee had experimentally determined the balancing characteristics of numerous classes of tank and tender locomotive of the four main-line railways. Previously, railway civil engineers had tended to accept or reject tentative locomotive designs merely with reference to their dead weight. Relatively little consideration was given to their likely dynamic impact at speed, which could bear little relation to dead weight. One interesting discovery was that the 'River' had the lightest hammerblow values of any of the major two-cylinder designs (with outside cylinders) investigated. As a result, at *high* rotational speeds its combined axleload, ie static axleload plus hammerblow, was little greater than that of the smaller HR 'Castle' and 'Clan' 4-6-0s (see Appendix).

In view of this revelation it is curious that a contemporary enthusiast was informed that the two Perth 'Rivers' had come off passenger workings early in 1917 because they allegedly pounded and damaged the track at speed! This accusation should surely havse been levelled at the Pickersgill 4-6-0s that succeeded them. The 'Rivers' must have incorporated only a minimal proportion of reciprocating balance and so one wonders as to their riding qualities at speed. Their attributes in this respect when fairly new are not known, but they were openly regarded as the best 4-6-0s on the Caledonian by the men, who of course had several such classes to choose from.

Despite the very desirable advantages of a 6in greater girth of boiler, and 7 extra tons resting on the coupled wheels compared to 'Clan', the latter were far from displaced by the belated appearance of their predecessors. In 1930 ten standard LMS 'Crab' 2-6-0s came into service between Perth and Inverness, which ultimately permitted the transfer of several 'Clans' to the Oban line even before the allocation of the very first batch of Stanier Class 5 4-6-0s to the Highland Section late in 1934.

The 'Rivers' do not appear to have made a dramatic impact north of Perth and the first to be withdrawn was No 14757, from Blair Atholl shed at the end of 1936. The remainder were soon divided between Perth and Dundee West sheds, the latter housing the last survivor, No 14758, in December 1939. This engine, along with No 14760, reprieved from the scrap road at Kilmarnock on account of the war, was sent to Ayr shed in 1941. Here they were popularly dubbed 'Gneisenau' and 'Scharnhorst' respectively after a highly regrettable contemporary naval incident. Coupled together they hauled very heavy empty troop trains aggregating up to 440 tons between Ayr and Stranraer. Always a weak feature, their steam reversers by now would only 'maintain' two settings — full gear, either forward or reverse. Their boilers still steamed excellently, however, and could meet the demands of maximum cut-off working at an average speed of about 20mph or less maintained over the 59-odd miles of mountainous grades to Stranraer. This required hard shovelling on the part of the fireman, and some drivers would insert wooden wedges into the bottom of the expansion links in order to enforce a measure of expansive working. By this time also there was no doubt as to their riding qualities; they lurched alarmingly down the banks, sometimes showering the footplate with coal. It was rumoured that they were eventually taken off these duties because of alleged damage to the track between Stranraer and Girvan, a curious echo of the 1917 story.

After the war both engines worked heavy coal trains between Dalmellington and Ayr. One day whilst so employed No 14758 failed when its nearside steamchest suddenly ruptured with a spectacular sunburst of steel. At Ayr shed the offending cylinder was blanked off, steam was raised for the last time, and the final journey to St Rollox cautiously was made on one cylinder. The remaining engine, No 14760, pottered about the Ayr district on local turns until it quietly disappeared in December 1946, seemingly arousing no comment despite the peculiar interest that always attached to these engines and to the fate of their designer.

After the First World War, contrary to popular belief, F. G. Smith did not become a consultant engineer, but set up in business with a friend as a steel merchant in Newcastle-upon-Tyne importing steel sections from Belgium for building work. F. G. Smith & Co had an office in Mawson's Buildings, 13 Mosley Street; this enterprise flourished for about eleven years, and closed down around 1933 on account of the imposition of heavy import duties and the generally depressed economic climate. A bitter blow had earlier fallen when the Smiths' only child, Stephen, obliged to accept a post overseas because of mass unemployment at home, died of blackwater fever within a few weeks of his arrival in Assam. For the last 20 years or so of his life Smith lived quietly off his private income, spending much time developing ingenious gadgets of a domestic nature. Cupboards would automatically become illuminated up on being opened, and he hinged his sash windows to open inward to facilitate cleaning, a feature of the house which survives to this day. He became very interested in long case clocks which he reconditioned. Smith never regained any connection with or real interest in railways, and died at home on February 25, 1956 in his 84th year.

HR No	Name	Date to traffic	CR No	LMS No	Withdrawn	Mileage at withdrawal
70	*River Ness*	9/1915 11/1915	938	14756	11/1939	674,028
(71)	*(River Spey)*	11/1915	939	14757	12/1936	587,953
(72)	*(River Tay)*	11/1915	940	14758	9/1945	715,992
(73)	*(River Findhorn)*	12/1915	941	14759	2/1939	623,809
(74)	*(River Garry)*	12/1915	942	14760	12/1946 (4/1939*)	737,826
(75)	*(River Tummel)*	1/1916	943	14761	11/1939	590,228

*reinstated 9/1940

CHAPTER FOUR

The 'Cumming' 4-6-0s

F. G. Smith's impromptu successor at Lochgorm was Christopher Cumming, late District Locomotive Superintendent, Burntisland, NBR. Cumming was quite elderly when he was called to the job. A man of genial disposition, he liked to make his footplate journeys seated in an armchair, so it is said, otherwise not a great deal is known about him. There is no strong evidence to support the belief held by some that he was related by marriage to William Whitelaw.

Cumming was essentially a locomotive running man who, whilst nominally responsible in reality, can have had little to do with the design of the 18 locomotives popularly ascribed to his name. Such credit is really due to the builders, Hawthorn Leslie & Co, and to some extent to the departed Smith. The erstwhile employment of two 'Castles' north of Inverness on the Farther North mail trains, or the more usual alternative of hauling these with 4-4-0s in pairs, were both luxuries the hard-pressed Highland could ill afford. Shortly before his untimely departure Smith envisaged a modern superheated 4-4-0, referred to as a 'superheated Loch', especially for the job. In August 1915 his ideas were communicated to NBL, Andrew Barclay & Co, and Hawthorn Leslie & Co in the form of a rough specification with the invitation to submit detailed proposals. Whether all three builders each submitted tentative designs is uncertain. Ironically at the same Board meeting on October 7 at which the disposal of the 'Rivers' was decided, Smith's resignation was accepted and Cumming's appointment was agreed, it was also 'resolved to contract with Messrs. Hawthorn Leslie & Co. for two 4-4-0 superheated engines with axle-weight limit of 17 tons'.

These duly arrived in November 1916 and were respectively numbered and named 73 *Snaigow* and 74 *Durn*. Actually slightly exceeding the specified axleload by 3cwt, these two engines must have reflected broadly what Smith had originally had in mind, having several features similar to those of the 'Rivers', i.e. Robinson superheater, Belpaire firebox, and outside cylinders with piston valves and Walschaerts valve gear. (The latter features were unprecedented in a British 4-4-0 and were to remain unique as far as British two-cylinder 4-4-0 practice was concerned.) These two engines were of a most distinctive appearance and set the general pattern for the subsequent goods and passenger 4-6-0 classes, which likewise were endowed with a similar roomy cab but with a noticeably extended roof, and had their valve gear largely concealed within an extension of the coupled wheel splashers. The pistons were provided with tail rods, but these were removed after a few years.

Incidentally, a register at the Mitchell Library, Glasgow indicates that NBL prepared two 4-4-0 schemes for the Highland Railway during September 1915, but no details of these appear to survive. Messrs Andrew Barclay, Sons & Co. Ltd. are unable to confirm whether or not they submitted a corresponding proposal during that period.

The three classes under discussion provided one of the very few instances of locomotives being designed as well as constructed by a contractor for a British main line railway. (Even in the celebrated case of the LMS 'Royal Scots' participation by the railway was far greater.) The head of the locomotive side of R. & W. Hawthorn Leslie & Co. (who were also shipbuilders on Tyneside) was W. C. Watson, who had formerly been Chief Draughtsman. Although commonly referred to as the General Manager, his official title was merely that of 'Works Manager'. To succeed Watson in the drawing office following his elevation in 1910 a remarkably young man of only 27 was appointed, John W. Hobson. Whilst Hobson would have taken considerable responsibility, the real credit for the three so-called 'Cumming' Highland Railway designs lay with a leading chargehand in the drawing office, one J. E. 'Jack' Armstrong, who was given a free hand.

In designing new superheater 4-6-0s for the HR in the wake of the 'River Affair' Armstrong displayed great skill in producing what were thoroughly up-to-date, powerful engines within the stringent weight limitations insisted upon by the line's Chief Engineer. Whilst perpetuating certain features of their saturated steam predecessors (and the 'Rivers'), such as the sloping grate with horizontal rear section, Armstrong made some innovations, e.g. a more even spacing of the coupled wheels, of which the centre pair were provided with thin flanges. A short stocky man with ginger hair, Armstrong's genial demeanour concealed an extremely violent temper and he was not one to be crossed on any account. He maintained an uncooperative attitude towards Hobson, to whom he referred as 'Hook' on account of the unpopular Chief Draughtsman's devious personality (he was said to owe his position to the good offices of freemasonry).

In 1919 Armstrong left to become Chief Engineer to the Scarab Oil Burning Co., with whom he secured the post of Chief Draughtsman for Robert Sutton. He had a high regard for Sutton, who had developed the distinctive footplate and splasher arrangements of the Highland engines; it can have been no mere coincidence that an HR 'Clan' 4-6-0 was later experimentally fitted up for oil firing on the Scarab system. Seeking more lucrative prospects, Armstrong soon moved on to a highly successful career as Sales Manager with a fire-fighting equipment firm, and had nothing further to do with locomotives.

During the early 1920s a crisis occurred at Forth Banks which put the 'River Affair' completely in the shade. An order had been received from a South American customer for twelve three-cylinder 2-6-2 suburban tank locomotives. The first engine was completed and weighed in working order and found to exceed the estimate by *several tons*. In the original calculations no allowance had been made for the water in the side tanks! Under Watson's unruffled supervision drastic reconstruction was carried out in order to keep within the required axleload. The side tanks were cut right back and the back end modified to accommodate a trailing bogie. Hawthorn Leslie lost heavily on the deal and a promised repeat order to utilise the spare pony trucks never followed. (Ironically, the resultant 2-6-4Ts proved highly successful and orders for 60 more soon went to other British builders.) Hobson went to pieces and rumour at the time had it that he had threatened to commit suicide. Unlike F. G. Smith he was to keep his job and died in harness as Technical Manager at Forth Banks early in 1948, almost 50 years after he had started there as an apprentice.

Had Smith remained it is reasonable to presume that he would sooner or later have turned his hand to producing a modern successor to the now ageing Jones 4-6-0s. A 5ft 3in 2-6-0 version of the *Snaigow* 4-4-0, having many major components in common, would probably have sufficed. As it was, with Smith gone and the desperate situation facing the Highland, it would not have been at all surprising if additional 'Big Goods' engines had appeared built to the old 1894 drawings. In the event a new 'Big Goods' was designed, dimensionally very similar to the old, but completely updated with superheater and piston valves.

Four of the new engines were authorised by the Board on February 28, 1917 at a cost of £6,957 each — specification 'subject to adjustment'. Newlands subsequently gave his blessing by expressing 'his approval and satisfaction of the design and weights of these engines'. He was given no grounds for complaint on this score, as the engines weighed only ½ton more than a Jones 4-6-0 and at 13.9tons they had the lightest axleload of any British 4-6-0 built.

On account of the war copper had become a very scarce commodity and several Highland engines had to be renewed with steel fireboxes during the course of heavy repairs. It was accordingly arranged that the last two of the new 4-6-0s should have steel, and the other two copper fireboxes. Notwithstanding, construction was prolonged and although they were dated 1917 delivery to Inverness did not begin until June of the following year, when it was immediately resolved to order a further four similar engines with steel or copper fireboxes.

The second series, all with copper fireboxes, arrived late in 1919. They were distinguished by a continuous splasher which ran from cylinders to cab, but surprisingly were equipped with screw reverse. Like the Jones 4-6-0s the earlier engines had lever reverse, much beloved in Scotland. Contrary to what has been written elsewhere and despite the tedium it incurred during shunting operations, the second series retained their screw reverse to the end. Furthermore, at least one of the lever engines (old No 75) was at some stage in its career also altered to screw. Latterday HR practice was to specify screw reverse for new passenger engines and this no doubt reflected the frequent employment of these 4-6-0s in passenger service when new, despite the fact they were ostensibly goods engines. At speed they developed an extremely pronounced 'fore-and-aft' motion owing to inadequate balancing, but they were always highly regarded by engine crews. Ambiguously referred to officially as the 'Big Goods' by the management, and more specifically as the 'Inverness Goods' by the builders, to the enginemen they were the 'Superheaters' simply because these were the first engines so fitted that had ever regularly operated between Perth and Inverness. To the irritation of purists these attractive little 4-6-0s were often referred to in later years as the 'Clan Goods' on account of close resemblance to their larger and slightly later passenger counterparts, the 'Clan' class.

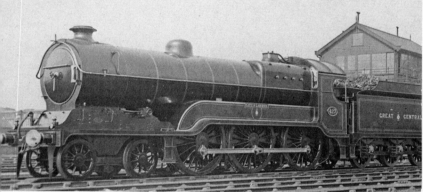

Top: McIntosh Caledonian Railway 6ft 6in 4-6-0 No 49 as originally built in 1903.
/Rixon Bucknall Collection

Centre: Robinson Great Central Railway superheated 6ft 9in passenger 4-6-0
No 427 *City of London* of 1913./*Ian Allan Library*

Bottom: North British Railway 4-4-2 passenger engine of 1906./*LPC*

HR Jones 'Big Goods' 4-6-0s

Top: A fine study of Jones 'Big Goods' 4-6-0 No 104 at Perth. The engine is practically as originally built, except that the tender was originally devoid of the initials 'HR'./*LPC*

Centre: The famous photograph of Jones 4-6-0 No 113 alleged to be in course of delivery from the makers at Stanley Junction./*Rixon Bucknall Collection*

Bottom: Jones 4-6-0 No 112 in the roundhouse at Inverness. The engine has had its smokebox wingplates removed at quite an early date./*LPC*

Top: Peace at last! 'Big Goods' 4-6-0 No 109 ascends Drumochter on a freight soon after the First World War in 1919.
/Locomotive & General Railway Photographs

Centre: A Jones 4-6-0 still in substantially original condition after 30 years, LMS No 17920 looks smart in plain black livery./*LPC*

Bottom: A 'Big Goods' ends its days on the Kyle line. The relatively small proportions of these engines by later standards is apparent in this photograph.
/Locomotive & General Railway Photographs

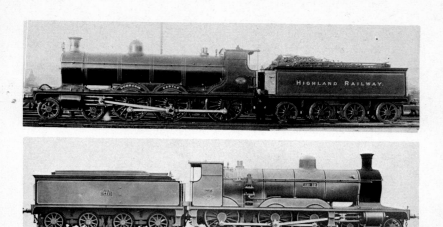

Top left: HR No 103 as originally restored by the LMSR in 1936./*Ian Allan Library*

Centre left: Repainted yellow and restored to working order No 103 pilots the 'Three Summits' Railtour at Auchinleck on June 30, 1963./*A. Swain*

Bottom left: HR No 103 at Perth in June 1962./*John K. Morton*

Highland 'Castles'

Top: HR No 142 *Dunrobin Castle* built in 1900, in orginal condition./*LPC*

Above: NBL photograph of one of the 50 'Castles' built in 1911 for the Etat system in France. Note the taller chimney and wider cab./*LPC*

Below: One of the four modified 'Castles' built by Smith in 1913, HR No 27 *Thurso Castle* traverses the Highland wastes./*Rixon Bucknall Collection*

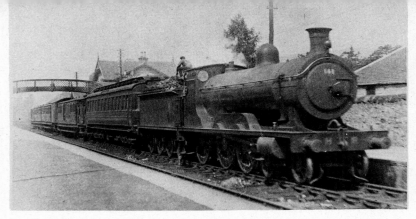

Above: An extremely rare action shot of HR No 141 *Ballindalloch Castle* with extended smokebox storming through Blair Atholl with an Inverness-Perth express in June 1915./*Kenn Nunn Collection/LCGB*

Below: Beaufort Castle under repair at Lochgorm Works in July 1915. Note the Smith-style number painted high on the cab side in place of the original brass numberplate contributed to the war effort./*Ken Nunn Collection/LCGB*

Bottom: HR No 50 *Brodie Castle,* one of the 6ft trio of 1917 with six-wheeled tenders. As originally built these engines had capuchon chimneys similar to those of the 1913 batch./*Rixon Bucknall Collection*

Above: Brodie Castle as LMS No 14691 storms out of Perth with a northbound train soon after the grouping./*Ian Allan Library*

Below: Beaufort Castle in LMS red livery fitted with short chimney./*LPC*

Bottom: Brahan Castle poses for an official portrait in 1928. The engine has acquired a Derby-pattern smokebox door, probably fitted at St Rollox who had recently built some Midland 4F 0-6-0s./*LPC*

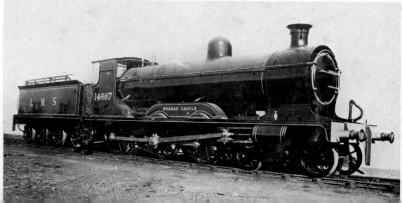

Top left: Gordon Castle as rebuilt in 1930 with boiler and extended smokebox ex-*Murthly Castle./F. Inglis*

Centre left: Darnaway Castle makes a spirited departure from Elgin on an Aberdeen-Inverness train composed of LNER stock. (One of the three 1917 engines, it latterly ran with a bogie tender.)/*F. R. Hebron*

Bottom left: Westinghouse-fitted *Beaufort Castle* at Slochd./*M. W. Earley*

The 'Rivers'

Above: The unfortunate designer of the 'River' class, F. G. Smith (left). A photograph believed to have been taken in 1910 in the Carriage Shops at Needlefield when Smith was Works Manager./*Author's collection*

Below: No known photograph exists of Smith HR 4-6-0 *River Ness* as originally built. Contrary to appearances the engine illustrated here is in reality the last of the series (HL 3100) *alias* CR No 943 (bottom), completed late in 1915.
/*South Tyneside Libraries*

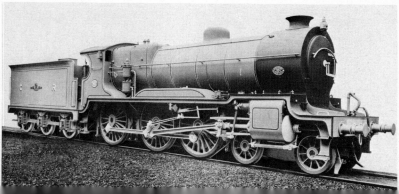

Top: HR No 70 *River Ness* as CR No 938 heads a down freight out of Carlisle. Note the handsome chimney./*Rixon Bucknall Collection*

Above: CR No 938 at St Rollox in October 1920. Note the embossed McIntosh-style number plate (also applied to 939); Nos 940-943 had Drummond-type inlaid plates./*Ken Nunn Collection/LCGB*

Below: The inspiration for the 'River' class, R. W. Urie's 6ft Class H15 mixed traffic 4-6-0 No 486 built at Eastleigh Works, LSWR, late 1913./*LPC*

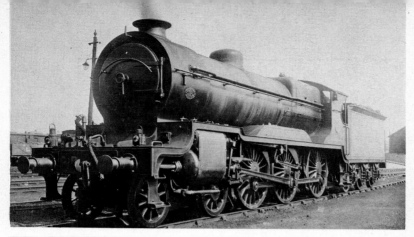

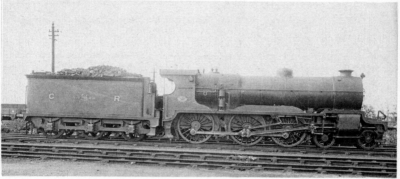

Above: Two views of one of the 'Rivers' delivered direct to the Caledonian Railway. The shorter and less pleasing flared chimney will be noted.
/Ian Allan Library & Rixon Bucknall Collection

Below: The final 'River', CR No 943, heads a fast freight out of Carlisle c.1922.
/H. Gordon Tidey

Above: A 'River' in Derby red. LMS No 14758 on shed soon after the grouping./*LPC*

Below: An interesting view of Perth Shed in 1939 with the former *River Ness* in the foreground shortly before withdrawal. Also in the picture are a Stanier 'Black Five', a 'Royal Scot', a Midland 'Compound' and a Pickersgill 'Greyback'./*F. Inglis*

Bottom: The exile's return. A 'River' in a Highland setting at Blair Atholl. (The only major LMS modification was removal of the cylinder tail rods.)/*M. W. Earley*

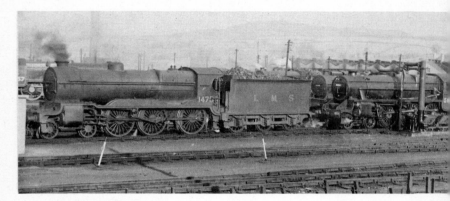

HR Superheater Goods 4-6-0s

Above: HR 4-4-0 No 73 *Snaigow,* one of the two 'Superheated Lochs' initiated by F. G. Smith but designed in detail and built by Hawthorn Leslie & Co in 1916 to work the North Mails to Wick./*Ian Allan Library*

Below: Newly arrived from the makers superheater goods 4-6-0 No 75 poses for the camera./*LPC*

Bottom: HR No 75 at Perth Shed./*Rixon Bucknall Collection*

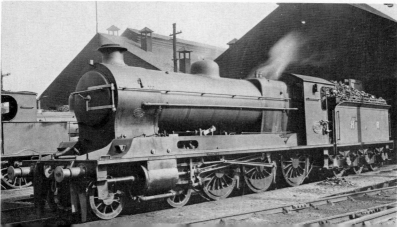

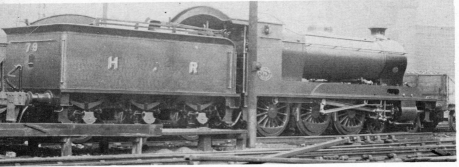

Top: The second of the 1919 series, HR No 80, hauls a freight on the single-track main line. Note the screw reverse./*LPC*

Above: Newly emerged from Forth Banks Works, brand new HR superheater goods 4-6-0 No 79, first of the modified 1919 quartet, stands outside Newcastle Central Station awaiting delivery in October 1919./*Ken Nunn Collection/LCGB*

Below: HR No 79 heads a freight near Luncarty./*Rixon Bucknall Collection*

Top: Showing a leg! In early LMS days superheater goods No 17951 heads north on a fine summer day near Luncarty./*LPC*

Above: Amid more typical Highland weather an unidentified superheater goods 4-6-0 pulls away from Lairg with a train for Inverness./*F. R. Hebron*

Below: Under public ownership. BR No 57954 stands at Kyle of Lochalsh. (The cylinder tail rods were removed by the LMS.)/*C. C. B. Herbert*

Above: No 57954 under repair in Lochgorm Works in May 1949./*P. B. Whitehouse*

Below: With the Isle of Skye in the background 57955 with CR-type chimney and snifting valve stands at Kyle of Lochalsh in August 1950. /*C. C. B. Herbert*

Bottom: No 57956 shunts at Kyle in August 1951./*W. J. V. Anderson*

In July 1917 the Highland Railway informed the Railway Executive Committee that it wished to order four superheated 4-6-0 passenger locomotives. The details of these were settled a few days later at a meeting held in Newcastle-upon-Tyne between Cumming, Newlands and Mr. Watson, who represented Hawthorn Leslie & Co. It is recorded that Newlands formally 'agreed to this engine' in a letter to a director the following week.

It is clear that Newlands now had a very strong say in matters concerning new locomotives. As with the 'goods' 4-6-0s, the builders played safe and produced virtually an updated version of a 6ft 'Castle' — or alternatively a 'watered down' 'River'! In fact the new design weighed only 2tons more than the final batch of 'Castles'; the extra weight, which must largely have been due to the superheater, resposed on the leading bogie. An interesting innovation was the provision of a cylindrical smokebox which rested on a cast saddle. This probably reflected the trouble which must have been experienced under adverse wartime maintenance conditions with poor steaming due to air leaks in the built-up smokeboxes of the earlier engines. The cylinders were cast to a similar pattern to those of the two 4-4-0s and the 'goods' 4-6-0s. The 10in piston valves were, therefore, situated on the same vertical centre lines as the cylinders. The Walschaerts valve gear actuated directly a dummy 'lay spindle', the motion of which was transmitted via a short arm to the valve spindle proper. The author can think of no logical explanation for the adoption of this curious feature.

All three of the Highland/Hawthorn Leslie locomotive classes were designed to conform with a composite loading gauge which was dictated not only by the more generous Highland gauge, but also by limitations of the North Eastern and Caledonian systems. The engines would inevitably have had to traverse NER metals on leaving the makers and presumably were routed via Carlisle, whence the Caledonian would convey them to Perth. The first 'Clan' arrived at Inverness during April 1919, when it was discovered that its original estimated cost of £8,059 had been substantially exceeded by £957. Nevertheless, the engine must have given every satisfaction, for the directors were very soon enquiring as to the purchase of a second batch of eight 'Clans' (ie in addition to those already in course of delivery). On being informed by Hawthorn Leslie that the unit cost would be an inflated £11,105, they settled for only four engines, which were delivered during 1921.

In addition to the problem of rising costs, suitable locomotive coal was becoming a scarce and expensive commodity. The HR had traditionally employed Fife steam coal, but at this time the country was being forced to import a great deal of its coal. Hence, in October 1920, the conversion of 4-6-0 No 53 *Clan Stewart* to oil-firing on the Scarab patent system was authorised at an estimated cost of £500.

No 53 was the only 'Clan' to be stationed at Inverness, the other three being at Perth. Its oil was carried in five former gas storage tanks (removed from carriages on the latter's conversion to electric lighting) which were mounted on the top of the tender. There was a single burner in the firebrick-lined steel firebox, with a maximum capacity of 220gall of oil/hr, the fuel having a calorific value of 18,900BThU/lb.

Will Tulloch was brought up from Perth for the tests of No 53, which took place during the early part of 1921. On its initial trial trip the engine took 420 tons out to Forres and back unassisted, but subsequently, during through runs between Perth and Inverness, it was given more moderate loadings, again without assistance over Slochd and Drumochter summits. Consumption was 31lb to the mile, and of the 460gall consumed in total, 70gall were attributed to standby losses on one particular run, when the engine took 293tons from Perth to Aviemore, and 241tons from Aviemore to Inverness. The duration of the 118mile run was 3hr 54min, including four stops.

Just as these trials were coming to a conclusion other British railways were equipping many locomotives as oil burners because of the Coal Strike, but no more HR conversions took place. The second batch of 'Clans' arrived as coal burners.

This second series were distinguished by a lighter plain green livery and a subtle alteration to the splashers. They also had copper fireboxes, as the original steel boxes in the 1919 series had not proved satisfactory. Because of ill health Cumming resigned early in 1922 as suddenly as he had originally been appointed, and was succeeded in office by David Chalmers Urie, a son of R. W. Urie of Eastleigh. Soon after his arrival and upon making his first tour of inspection Urie was astonished to find all four of the 1919 'Clans' deliberately concealed in the dark recesses of Aviemore carriage shed, stored unserviceable with burnt fireboxes. These were promptly despatched to Lochgorm for overhaul and repainting. The offending steel fireboxes were probably replaced then also, although those in Nos 77 and 78 enjoyed a life of eight or nine years.

Urie found much evidence of slack discipline in the Locomotive Department after the rigours of the war. Of small stature, he was not a man to court popularity. In 1923 he instituted through working of the 'Large Ben' 4-4-0s between Inverness and Wick, and of the 'Clans' between Inverness and Glasgow (Buchanan Street). These workings did not persist for very long but they attracted particular venom from the footplate fraternity as they were lodging turns requiring the crews to spend nights away from home. Urie was once unwittingly referred to in the hearing of his own brother as an 'Irish blackguard', which would have been a much stronger sentiment then than now. (Although a Scot, Urie had come to Lochgorm from the Midland Great Western Railway).

The 'Clans' performed very much in the manner of the 'Castles'. Decidedly rough to ride on, they steamed well and pulled hard on the banks, but their short lap/short travel piston valves proved a handicap to free fast running on the level. The weakest feature of the 'Clan' was its main frame, which was notoriously prone to cracking. The 1⅛in thickness was the same as in the 'Castles' and larger 'Rivers', which evidently did not suffer so markedly. The 'Castle' had smaller cylinders and shallower frames, but by Highland standards the 'River' probably had led a more cosseted existence in its earlier years. The 'Clans' were worked very hard throughout their lives and their relatively light frames were undoubtedly inadequate to withstand the prolonged powerful thrusts of two 21in cylinders at late cut-offs. In this connection it is interesting to note that the two superheated Glasgow & South Western 4-6-0s which had the same cylinder dimensions and boilers of very similar size (see Chapter 10) were provided with frames 1¼in thick compared to the 1⅛in of their saturated predecessors.

The 'Clans' had an unusually high power to weight ratio and weighed 12 tons less than a Pickersgill Caledonian '60' 4-6-0 (which also fell in the LMSR Power Class 4P range) at the opposite extreme. Indeed the Highland engine, as regards weight and its distribution, was very similar to Pickersgill's smaller special Oban 4-6-0. In 1934 'Clans' *Fraser, Munro, Mackinnon* and *Cameron* began working over the Oban line and were joined a little later by the remaining engines just displaced from the Highland main line by the newly arrived Stanier Class 5 4-6-0s. Distributed between Balornock, Stirling and Oban sheds for the next five years, the 'Clans' performed their hardest and best work, although proving somewhat lethargic between Glasgow and Stirling.

Officially limited to 255 tons unassisted as against the 230 tons of the Pickersgill 4-6-0 (Class 3P), in practice the 'Clans' were very often loaded up to 300 tons. In the *Railway Magazine* for January 1938 O. S. Nock mentions *Clan Chattan* hauling 302tons tare (315tons gross) up the 5 miles of 1 in 60 between Balquhidder and Glenoglehead at 17mph. Simple calculations suggesat that in order to achieve this heroic effort the engine must have been worked at or very near full forward gear, with the boiler evaporating steam at the limit of its capacity.

In the summer of 1939 the Class 5 appeared in strength on the Oban line and the 'Clans' promptly returned to their home ground. They subsequently made occasional appearances at Kyle of Lochalsh and Wick, but their days were numbered and withdrawal commenced in 1943. Having spent its last years at Aviemore and finally Inverness, mainly employed on goods trains, the last survivor, *Clan Mackinnon,* made its final run as BR No 54767 under its own steam from Balornock to Kilmarnock for breaking up on February 4, 1950. Despite the lean build of the 'Clan' it is a curious fact that not one of the more robust 'Rivers' equalled the *average* total mileage of the former, which probably goes to show how little the 'Rivers' were exploited during their comparatively short lives.

The little superheater goods 4-6-0 withstood the onslaught of the Class 5 until after World War 2. When tested over the Oban line in 1933 it came off second best to the 'Clan', but its own special preserve was the picturesque Dingwall and Skye line. On this its relatively small driving wheels and short rigid wheelbase proved ideal to cope with the abounding severe gradients, which included the 1 in 50 ascents in both directions to Ravens Rock, and the sinuous curves along the shores of Loch Carron. As a result of some bridge strengthening these engines first appeared at Kyle of Lochalsh in 1928 and were an integral part of the local scene there for over the next 20 years.

A little documented class, the eight 'Superheaters' were remarkable for the number of minor variations between individual engines, some of which have already been mentioned. In later years some acquired CR-type chimneys and snifting valves. A notable event was the fitting of No 17951 with a new boiler in June 1939. A total of five new boilers were built and fitted at St Rollox up to 1944, but only Nos 17953 and 17957 were scrapped carrying their original boilers. No 17952, reboilered in 1939, was scrapped only seven years later and its boiler put on to No 17954, whose 1942 boiler duly passed secondhand to No 17956.

These little 4-6-0s performed yeoman service over the hard-pressed Kyle road during wartime, but soon after hostilities ceased preparations were made to permit use of the Class 5. Following enlargement of the turntable at Kyle the Stanier engines duly arrived in 1948, but a 'Superheater' was generally still to be seen at Kyle right up to the end, which occurred late in 1952. Some of the last survivors operated from Inverness on local goods trains, mainly to Keith, to Dingwall and Tain, and over the Black Isle branch. Sometimes they would pilot the mail from Dingwall to Achnasheen, or work a local passenger turn to Tain. Although rated in Power Class 4, with a total weight roughly equalling that resting on the coupled wheels of a Stanier Class 5, not to mention a factor of adhesion of only 3.6, they prompted an observer very familiar with these handsome machines in their final post-war years to remark to the author that in his experience on their home ground they displayed a greater haulage capacity than the 'Black Five'!

HR No	Maker's No	Delivery date	LMS No	New boiler fitted	Date scrapped
75	3286	6/1918	17950	1/1940	8/1950
76	3287	/1918	17951	6/1939	5/1951
77	3288	/1918	17952	12/1939	10/1946
78	3289	/1918	17953	—	10/1948
79	3371	10/1919	17954	3/1942	10/1952
80	3372	10/1919	17955	/1944	6/1952
81	3373	11/1919	17956	(6/1947)	3/1952
82	3374	11/1919	17957	—	3/1946

HR No	Name	Maker's No	Delivery date	LMS No	Date scrapped	Mileage at withdrawal
49	Clan Campbell	3329	4/1919	14762	6/1947	822,393
51	Clan Fraser	3330	/1919	14763	8/1944	Not known
52	Clan Munro	3331	5/1919	14764	4/1948	801,426
53	Clan Stewart	3332	6/1919	14765	1/1945	789,191
54	Clan Chattan	3443	/1921	14766	3/1944	726,877
55	Clan Mackinnon	3444	7/1921	14767	2/1950	808,868
56	Clan Mackenzie	3445	7/1921	14768	3/1945	732,699
57	Clan Cameron	3446	/1921	14769	10/1943	750,969

All the 'Clans' were dual-fitted c. 1923-c. 1936.

CHAPTER FIVE

A Locomotive Legend

"Already the third year of the twentieth century constitutes an epoch in the history of locomotive engineering . . . and now it witnesses a new and remarkable departure on the Caledonian Railway."[*] So wrote Charles Rous-Marten a fortnight after the emergence of J. F. McIntosh's first 6ft 6in 4-6-0 passenger engine from St Rollox Works on March 17, 1903.

Numbered 49, it ran initial trials between Edinburgh and Glasgow in drab shop grey before returning to works after a few weeks to receive a coat (or rather, several coats plus varnish) of Caledonian blue paint fully lined out and the exceptionally large initials CR applied to the sides of its large bogie tender. A second engine, No 50, appeared the following month and ran trials between Glasgow and Perth before repainting and receiving the name *Sir James Thompson* after the current CR Chairman and erstwhile General Manager. In due course No 50 was sent south to the Caledonian shed at Carlisle. This shed was then still known as Etterby, but was renamed to the now more familiar Kingmoor in 1915 to avoid verbal confusion with Upperby (LNWR) amid the intense wartime through traffic.

No 49, however, remained in Glasgow and was stationed at Polmadie to work the CR prestige express, the 'Corridor' diner which left Glasgow Central at 2pm for Carlisle; it returned on the 8.16pm ex-Carlisle. At the turn of the century the up 'Corridor' was the heaviest express regularly worked over British metals. Furthermore, it followed an exacting route which attained a maximum altitude of 1015ft at Beattock Summit, on the reverse or northbound approach to which a banker was almost invariably provided at Beattock itself. This latter assisted over the 10 miles to Summit, up an average gradient of 1 in 81. At its lightest loading, about 300 tons, the 'Corridor' would fall within the compass of a 'Dunalastair III' 4-4-0, if the conditions were dry and fine, but by 1903 loadings often approached 400 tons and conditions in the Lowther Hills are often windy and wet. The Caledonian Board viewed unfavourably the practice of double-heading widely resorted to by its southern partner, the LNWR, and so the two new 4-6-0s were authorised in November 1902 at a cost of approximately £3,000 apiece.

Compared to a 'Dunalastair III' 4-4-0, the new six-coupled engines developed 36 per cent more tractive effort for an 18 per cent increase in grate area. Initially some doubt existed as to just how large the new engines really were. Rous-

---

[*] *The Engineer*, April 3, 1903 p.331

Marten originally stated the boiler was the same as that of the '600' class 0-8-0s (grate area 23sq ft) whilst *The Locomotive* quoted a grate of 31sq ft! Similarly the engine weight was initially given as 72 tons, but later as only 70 tons. On paper Nos 49 and 50 were easily the most powerful passenger engines in Great Britain at that time, simply because they combined the largest cylinders, 21in by 26in, with the highest boiler pressure, 200lb, then to be encountered in British practice. Rous-Marten quickly expressed doubt and later categorically claimed that in reality the cylinders were not actually bored out to 21in, which was simply a possible maximum figure. Certainly, although potent, this formidable combination soon proved to be too powerful for the locomotives' own good. In addition to obviating double-heading it had originally been hoped or intended to dispense with banking assistance on Beattock, but after a year or so a banker was invariably provided.

CR Passenger Locomotive Development 1896-1906

Type	'Dun I'	'Dun II'	'Dun III'	'Dun IV'	'49'	'903'
Wheel arrangement	4-4-0	4-4-0	4-4-0	4-4-0	4-6-0	4-6-0
Year Introduced	1896	1897	1899	1904	1903	1906
Cylinders (in)	18¼ x 26	19 x 26	19 x 26	19 x 26	21 x 26	20 x 26
Driving wheel diameter	6ft 6in	6ft 6in	6ft 6in	6ft 6in	6ft 6in	6ft 6in
Boiler pressure (lb)	160	175	180	180	200	200
Total heating surface (sq ft)	1,403	1,500	1,540	1,615	2,323	2,266
Grate area	20·6	20·6	22·0	21·0	26·0	26·0
Adhesion weight (tons)	31·25	32·7	34·65	37·75	53·5	54·5
Engine weight (tons)	47·0	49·0	51·7	56·5	70·0	73·0
Tractive effort (lb)	15,100	17,900	18,400	18,400	25,000	22,700

Nos 49 and 50 were really logical enlargements of the 'Dunalastair IV' 4-4-0, the first of which did not actually appear until over a year later, in May 1904. Having an identical girth of boiler barrel and hence very similar free gas area values, compared to the simple free-steaming 4-4-0 boiler that of the 4-6-0 had tubes of the same bore yet 50 per cent longer at 17ft 3in and a firegrate 24 per cent larger. Add in the longer shallow sloping grate, more difficult to fire than the short deep inter-axle firebox of the 4-4-0, and the attendant restricted rear ashpan (the Achilles heel of many an Edwardian locomotive), and the result is a locomotive which could not have been expected to put up a sustained performance commensurate with its large size.

Notwithstanding a good run recorded by Rous-Marten behind No 49 when new in the summer of 1903 (see Chapter 9), it was evidently felt that there was still room for considerable improvement. At the beginning of 1904, after less than one year in traffic, Nos 49 and 50 returned to St Rollox for heavy repairs during which the smokebox tubeplate, already slightly recessed, was pushed back substantially further into the boiler barrel to reduce the tube length to 15ft 8in. Within a few days of No 49's first appearance a correspondent to *The Engineer* had criticised the engine's excessively long boiler and tubes. He had dismissed the front 4ft or so of the barrel as non-productive dead weight and advocated setting back the smokebox by that amount, citing Belgian precedents as to appearance.

As well as arousing considerable interest the engines had evoked astonishment at the retention of inside cylinders in locomotives of such large size. Certainly the 9½in by 9½in driving axleboxes very soon showed signs of taking heavy punishment and so the cylinders were linered down at the same time to 20in (if they were not already of this bore). Richardson balanced slide valves were fitted in place of the original plain variety above the cylinders, and there is a suggestion that the boiler pressure of No 49 was reduced to 175lb.

Soon after these purely internal alterations had been made, No 49 appeared in Dundee on April 9, 1904 to work a football special to Parkhead, Glasgow, in an operation mounted to take a bit of wind out of rival North British sails. Almost exactly a year later the same engine worked further up the East Coast to Aberdeen for the first time on April 6, 1905, at the head of a 250ton special train composed of brand new St Rollox-built luxurious 12-wheel passenger stock, in anticipation of a new Glasgow-Edinburgh-Aberdeen service to be inaugurated four days later with 4-4-0s. During the course of the run J. F. McIntosh proposed the name 'Grampian Express' for the new train, which happy inspiration was immediately adopted. Hopes for a stirring return run were dashed by signal stops, but it was reported that despite strong winds 'on several occasions the speed reached quite 80 miles an hour'.

Despite the limelight attaching to No 49 at the expense of No 50 (simply because it was the Glasgow engine), No 49 a little later became notorious, being prone to run hot, unlike its identical sister. From the beginning it was obliged to make more frequent visits to the shops and in July 1906 it received new cylinders. No 49 is said to have lain out of use for almost a year at Bolornock prior to being superheated — not what one would have expected of a relatively new 4-6-0 in 1911! Nevertheless these two engines were of immeasurable publicity value to the Caledonian, even if at times it was misleadingly implied that they ranged the length of the West Coast Route down to Euston itself! They were the very embodiment of Edwardian locomotive elegance. To those who deplore modern standards of workmanship, it may come as a surprise to learn that only a few months after the construction of Nos 49 and 50, 150 St Rollox men were dismissed for slackness, a malaise that also afflicted at least one private locomotive manufacturer south of the Border at that period.

As well as solving some problems the new 4-6-0s created others, mainly by reason of their great length. No existing turntable on the Caledonian could take their 56ft 10½in total wheelbase and at Carlisle engine and tender had to be uncoupled and turned separately. In Glasgow they were either sent tender-first round the Cathcart Circle line or turned on the track triangle at Rutherglen. The installation of new 70ft turntables at Carlisle, Perth, Dundee and Aberdeen by early 1906 signalled the way for additional ten-wheeled passenger engines.

During the latter half of 1905 there were rumours in the popular railway press that the appearance of an Atlantic was imminent on the Caledonian Railway. At this time McIntosh was seriously considering construction of a few inside-cylinder 4-4-2s for service between Perth and Aberdeen; they were actually authorised but were not proceeded with. This proposal was quite distinct from the now fairly well-known de Glehn four-cylinder compound 4-4-2 project of

March 1905, first illustrated in the *Railway Magazine* for January 1942. This latter does not appear to have been very seriously mooted. Whilst extremely elegant it would probably have been a most ineffectual machine in the harsh realities of Caledonian life; weighing 15½ tons more than the largest existing 4-4-0s, its adhesive weight would have been 1¼ tons less. Five years later, whilst writing in *Cassier's Magazine* for March 1910 on 'British Express Locomotives', McIntosh heartily denounced the Atlantic type, which he claimed 'had not been a conspicuous success anywhere' and which he rejected on account of its limited adhesive capacity and alleged heating troubles associated with the carrying axle.

On the subject of compounding he remarked that 'the four-cylinder compound has worked well abroad, though it seems likely that some of its best work is done when running as a four-cylinder simple'. Whilst conceding that the use of outside cylinders had 'apparently some decided advantages' McIntosh concluded that the 'greater steadiness of running' of the inside-cylinder engine 'due to the closeness of the centres of cylinders, probably balances all its other defects'.

In his article, which did not always square with his own practices, McIntosh displayed a firm if sometimes biased grasp of the essentials of contemporary design and operation. Probably the most telling remark in the whole, profusely illustrated article was that 'efficiency and reliability are more to a locomotive superintendent than economy in fuel, and those who provide public facilities are wise not to take risks for the sake of small gains.' Such practical wisdom befitted a man who had first mounted the footplate 45 years earlier as a fireman and had since risen steadily to the top, despite the early loss of his right arm in an accident.

Rejection of the 4-4-2 type was followed in the summer of 1906 by more 4-6-0s, of which five, numbered 903 to 907, were put into traffic between May and July. A study of the drawings of these shows that valuable lessons had been learnt from Nos 49 and 50. A better balance was sought between cylinder demand and boiler capacity by reducing the diameter of the cylinders and increasing that of the boiler. The reduction in the size of the cylinders enabled these to be pitched 1¼ in closer together at 2ft 0¼ in centres, which in conjunction with a degree of dishing of the driving wheel centre castings, enabled the driving axlebox dimensions to be enlarged to 9½ in by 10½ in. Similarly the unnecessarily restricted coupled axle bearings of Nos 49 and 50 were greatly enlarged, giving a total increase in bearing surface of the order of 30 per cent. Whilst the total engine wheelbase remained unchanged the crank axle was moved 4in further back and the length of the connecting rod was correspondingly increased by that amount to 7ft. A built-up type crank axle superseded the solid forged pattern of the two 1903 engines.

The 1906 engines weighed 3 tons more than those of 1903 largely on account of the larger diameter boiler, partly to offset which the main frames were reduced in thickness from 1⅛ in to 1¹/₁₆ in. The new boilers had a maximum girth of 5ft 3½ in and were constructed in no fewer than four rings of decreasing diameter towards the smokebox, the tubeplate of which was recessed into the front ring; for some reason tube length increased once more to 16ft 8in. The 1903 boilers had been built in only three rings, with the smallest diameter in the centre, and had a main bank of 257 1¾in tubes supplemented by 13 2½in tubes in the bottom rows, which were more likely to become choked with ash. The latter sensible practicality, which also applied to the subsequent 'Dunalastair IV' 4-4-0s, was not repeated in Nos 903-7; they had 242 tubes of a uniform 2in diameter, which would in modern parlance, however, have given a more ideal A/S (gas area/surface) ratio.

McIntosh was anxious to save weight where he could and in the firebox the heavy girder stays of Nos 49 and 50 were replaced by direct stays that were screwed into the centre ¾in thick crown portion of the outer wrapper, which was rivetted to the two ⁵/₈in side sheets. This mode of construction featured in all subsequent 4-6-0s built at St Rollox, except the four large three-cylinder engines of 1921. The two 1903 4-6-0 boilers were the first constructed at St Rollox of such a girth that the traditional method of inserting the inner firebox through the bottom of the outer box was precluded. For this reason the backplate was outwardly flanged, Crewe-style, to facilitate rivetting, but this feature was never again repeated in subsequent large boilers fabricated at St Rollox.

A decidedly odd and seemingly hitherto unremarked feature of McIntosh's non-superheater engines which must have adversely affected both their steaming and general efficiency was that their blastpipe centres were deliberately set forward of the chimney axis. In the 4-6-0s this varied from ½in in the 5ft 'Oban' engines to a curiously precise ¹³/₁₆in in the big 6ft 6in passenger locomotives. This strange procedure is difficult to reconcile with McIntosh's remark in his 1910 article that 'the form of the nozzle (ie blastpipe) and its setting to the chimney may make all the difference between success and failure in automatically controlling steam production.' At the other end of the boiler another weak feature of many of his larger engines was inadequate ashpan capacity. In the 1906 6ft 6in 4-6-0s obvious pains were taken to try and get more air to the rear portion of the grate behind the trailing coupled axle, a region which must rapidly have become blanked off by accumulated ash in the two earlier engines.

Only the first of the five new 4-6-0s, No 903, was for some curious reason named after the estate of a director who later became Deputy Chairman (see Chapter 12). Like *Dunalastair* of ten years earlier, *Cardean* was an obscure locale in the wilds of Perthshire soon to become a household name emblazoned in letters of gold on splashers of blue. The engine was destined to become the most famous individual locomotive in Scotland and to become a legend in its own lifetime. When run in it took over the working of the 'Corridor' from No 49, which it then regularly worked, except for disappearances during repair (when No 49 sometimes then deputised), for ten years. After about three or four years it was fitted with a highly distinctive deep-toned hooter, more reminiscent of a contemporary Cunarder, which was supplied by Colonel Denny, a Dumbarton shipbuilder who was a director on the Caledonian Board. Such was the prestige attaching to the engine by this time that in 1910 the CR ordered 30,000 tinplate clockwork 1¼in-gauge models of No 903 from Bassett-Lowke Ltd; they sold for half a crown each. Such were the numbers produced that a few must surely survive in attics to this day, and a specimen of this very passable model can be seen at the Museum of Childhood in Edinburgh.

CR No 903 was originally driven by Will Currie of Polmadie shed, who was promoted to Locomotive Inspector soon after surviving the alarming crank axle failure related in Chapter 11. He was succeeded by David Gibson, with whom the *Cardean* legend is synonomous. The fame of No 903 resided not in dazzling exploits, of which there was probably ever only one (which could well have been the most outstanding effort by a British locomotive using saturated steam, see Chapter 9), but in the regularity with which it worked the 'Corridor', identifiable to the public by its name, however obscure was the latter's origins.

Without this accolade No 903 could well have been as little known as its four identical sisters, which gained relatively little limelight. When brand new No 905 was initially allocated to Dalry Road shed, Edinburgh and mainly worked the 2pm Princes St-Carlisle, returning with the Edinburgh portion of the down 'Corridor'. Its driver was Will Stavert, who the previous year had coaxed a stupendous effort out of the pioneer 'Dunalastair IV' 4-4-0 No 140. Unfortunately for posterity Stavert's achievements with No 905 have gone unrecorded, although he was given little opportunity because loadings did not justify the big 4-6-0, which very soon moved to Perth to join No 904, displacing No 906 to Carlisle.

The two Perth engines led a leisurely existence, working alternatively the 11.40am Perth-Aberdeen and the 5.30pm Aberdeen-Perth one week and the 3.20pm Perth-Aberdeen, returning initially with the 7.50pm 'sleeper' and later with the 8pm fish train ex-Aberdeen, the next week. This represented a daily mileage of only 180, with the engines standing idle for all but about four hours of each day. During World War I two regular crews were assigned to each of the engines, which then additionally worked in a daily visit to Glasgow, thereby increasing their daily mileage to 300 miles or so. On top of this schedules did not demand a great deal of them. The 10am Glasgow-Perth non-stop was allowed 85min, and yet during the brief period the two Perth-based 'Rivers' were engaged in passenger service the latter could run Buchanan Street-Perth in just over 75min *with four stops*, at Larbert, Stirling, Dunblane and Gleneagles!

The two Carlisle engines, Nos 906 and 907, between them worked the down morning 'Postal' to Glasgow, returning on the 10am Central-Euston express, or on the 5.15am 'sleeper' from Carlisle to Glasgow, returning with 10.10am Glasgow-Manchester and Liverpool express. This represented a daily mileage of only about 200 miles, occupying about 5 hours of each day. Although the exploits of the two Perth engines went almost unrecorded, the ill-fated No 907 in its very early days appears to have put up some good performances as indicated in Chapter 9.

The arrival of the 1906 4-6-0s resulted in No 50 moving from Carlisle to Balornock, whence it made a daily round trip to Perth, commencing with the 2pm ex-Buchanan Street and returning on the 7.45pm Perth-Glasgow Central. Whilst idling at Perth a local turn to Dundee was worked in, bringing its daily mileage up to around 170. Latterly this engine operated in a 'link' with Pickersgill 4-6-0s Nos 60 and 956 on Glasgow-Perth workings.

Sister engine No 49 was at Polmadie throughout its Caledonian career and following the appearance of No 903 *Cardean* on the up and down 'Corridor', it was put on the heaviest Glasgow-Liverpool workings as far as Carlisle, although later it was extensively employed on fitted freights to Carlisle on account of its persistent heating troubles. After ten years *Cardean* in its turn came off the 'Corridor' during the winter of 1916-17 and for a time worked the Liverpool expresses, but latterly it worked in a 'link' with its successor, Pickersgill 4-6-0 No 61, on a morning train to Edinburgh and an afternoon express to Carlisle.

Between February and July 1911 all seven 6ft 6in 4-6-0s had been equipped with 24-element Schmidt superheaters. The first to be so treated was No 907, which ran its trials sporting a grey-painted boiler and blue underparts. New cylinders were also provided, having 8in diameter trick-ported wide ring piston valves. It was not necessary to increase the boiler pitch to accommodate these and so appearance was scarcely altered, except for the tell-tale damper cylinder on the right-hand side of the smokebox and the Wakefield mechanical lubricator mounted on the footplate ahead of the leading drive wheel splasher.

Contemporary observers detected no discernible improvement in performance, but the superheaters certainly must have made life a good deal easier for the firemen. Coal consumption was dramatically reduced, not least perhaps because the blastpipe would now be correctly centred with the chimney! The front-end arrangements closely followed that of the superheated 'Dunalastair IV' 4-4-0 No 139 of July 1910, which had been designed with the assistance of the Schmidt Superheater Company. St Rollox subsequently favoured the Robinson superheater, which became standard, and it is interesting to note that in 1914 the German enterprise commenced legal action for infringement of patent rights against J. G. Robinson. The eventual outcome, if any, in view of the turn of international events is not known. Dr Schmidt himself died in 1924.

The provision of superheaters and new cylinders in the big 6ft 6in 4-6-0s increased their weight by 1¼-1½ tons. About 55 tons represented the maximum that could be tolerated on six coupled wheels in McIntosh's time and late in 1913, shortly before his retirement, he outlined a Pacific. This in itself was quite remarkable for a man whose railway career had begun back in 1860 when a boy of 14. It is very doubtful if the engine could ever have been built before McIntosh's departure in February 1914 and just as well for his reputation that it was not. Even McIntosh would not have built an inside-cylinder Pacific and his projected 4-6-2 would have had four 16in by 26in cylinders with divided drive. The slender tapered boiler would have had two of the indifferent features of the large 4-6-0s to an even greater degree, ie long tubes (22ft) and a comparatively small firebox which would have afforded only 37sq ft of grate and lacked a combustion chamber. The McIntosh Pacific would have been a most elegant machine, but doubtless like the 4-6-0s it would rarely have lived up to its theoretical potential in everyday service. An illustration and dimensional particulars of this engine are to be found on p.138-9 of O. S. Nock's book *The Caledonian Railway* (Ian Allan 1962).

One suspects that this engine was conceived merely to keep one better than the LNWR, who earlier in the year had introduced the 'Claughton' four-cylinder

4-6-0s. As it was, the big 6ft 6in 4-6-0s were not unduly hard pressed. Indeed at the end of its independent existence Caledonian policy was to favour employment of the 4-4-0 wherever possible, if necessary in pairs, thereby reverting to the very situation which the original 4-6-0s had been built to avert nearly 20 years earlier. The institution of the 8-hour day in February 1919 had rendered it no longer feasible regularly to work specific trains with a particular locomotive handled by the same engine crews. Passenger 4-6-0s now worked in 'links' of two and three on particular turns in rotation, but the evident preference for 4-4-0s once again, even if it meant double-heading, must have reflected quite a measure of dissatisfaction with the 4-6-0 type.

After the grouping McIntosh's masterpieces rapidly faded away. Latterly shorn of their wingplates the two 1903 engines survived the later-built machines, which somehow contrived to retain this striking feature to the end. This was probably because both of the former had been renewed around 1924 with new main frames and new cylinders of slightly modified design. Painted black in their final years, they ended up at Perth and worked stopping trains to Aberdeen.

Thirty or so years later a preservation society would undoubtedly have sprung up to save *Cardean*, but the economic climate was hardly conducive to the restoration of even a national gem and the engine passed to the breaker's yard almost unnoticed. In its September 1932 issue the *Railway Magazine* suggested that upon withdrawal this locomotive should be preserved, blissfully unaware that it had already been cut up in mid-December 1930.

CHAPTER SIX

The McIntosh 5ft and 5ft 9in 4-6-0s

Whereas the real justification for certain of the numerous St Rollox 4-6-0 classes might be questioned, one that certainly earned its keep was the first of all which had already seen several months service by the time Nos 49 and 50 appeared on the scene.

Although only recently reboilered (1898-1901), the ten small Brittain 4-4-0s built specially in 1882 to work the newly opened Callander & Oban Railway were quite inadequate to handle the heavy corridor passenger stock ushered in with the new century. The light construction of some of the bridges precluded the use of a larger 4-4-0 because of axleload restrictions, thus dictating six coupled wheels in any new type; such an arrangement would also be of value in tackling the numerous short steep banks, and in providing adequate braking power on their descent. Even disregarding McIntosh's predeliction for inside cylinders, a 2-6-0 would not have been a likely candidate in 1902 and in any case the severe curvature of the Oban line would have militated against its probable 15-17ft of rigid wheelbase. Had McIntosh been a follower of contemporary American practice a 2-6-2 'Prairie' just might have presented a satisfactory solution, but in fact he produced a neat inside-cylinder 4-6-0 which simply amounted to a direct adaptation of his existing standards.

The new 4-6-0s were somewhat elongated hybrids of McIntosh's 4-4-0 passenger and 0-6-0 goods engines, having the leading bogie of the former and the six 5ft coupled wheels of the latter. The boiler was a direct development of that of both, necessarily elongated in the barrel and having a rather shallower grate. To get the engines round the curves without protest the coupled wheels were packed into the remarkably short wheelbase of 11ft 3in, only a little longer than that of some 4-4-0s, and the trailing axle was allowed ½in sideplay by virtue of a knuckle joint in the coupling rod. In order to accommodate the engines on existing turntables a short wheelbase tender was specially provided. Although engine and tender weighed 25 tons more than the little 4-4-0s (as newly rebuilt) which the new 4-6-0s superseded, the maximum axleload of the latter was scarcely one ton greater. Whereas the CR 6ft 6in 4-6-0s followed 4-4-0 practice in having the steam reverse gear located in the cab, in the 'Oban' and in later St Rollox 4-6-0 classes this was more sensibly bolted to the inside of the left-hand main frame plate directly adjacent to the valve gear it controlled and where it was reasonably accessible from the footplate.

Five of the new 4-6-0s, CR Nos 55-59, were turned out of St Rollox in mid-1902 and thereupon proceeded to monopolise the heaviest duties between Stirling and Oban for the next 20 years. With their small fireboxes and shallow grates they would not have beeng easy engines to fire and required skilful handling. Bearing this in mind and the fact that this difficult route demanded continually fluctuating rates of working, it was hardly to be expected that fuel consumption would be low. It is no doubt highly significant that in four additional engines built in 1905 (Nos 51-54) the tenders were provided with coal rails notwithstanding the renowned ability of Caley coal men to stack a tender well in excess of its officially stated capacity.

The second series closely resembled the first except that in line with the current St Rollox self-consciousness about excessive tube lengths the smokebox tubeplates were recessed 9in into the boiler barrel. Separate diagrams were issued in LMS days for the two boiler variants, but the same heating surface figures were always quoted for both, in contrast to the pedantic precision with which such dimensions were sometimes calculated to two decimal places elsewhere.

For photographic purposes one of the 1905 engines when new was misleadingly posed near St Rollox at the head of a rake of new 12-wheeled Edinburgh-Glasgow stock which would no more be seen at Oban than would a '55' in Edinburgh. However, one of the class, No 56, did later get farther afield when it was loaned to the Highland Railway in 1916. This engine was by far the largest and most modern locomotive the hard-pressed HR managed to acquire from elsewhere and perhaps for this reason did not return to the Caley fold until 1922. It appears to have been mainly used north of Inverness; soon after grouping sister engine No 55, as LMS 14600, worked for a while on the former Highland main line north of Perth.

Of the thirty new locomotives built at St Rollox during 1906, 20 were 4-6-0s. Furthermore, these were to three new designs, a common factor being four-ring boiler barrels having a maximum girth of 5ft 3½in as in the '903' class already described. Hard on the heels of the big passenger engines came five large-boilered versions of the 5ft 'Oban' 4-6-0s, CR Nos 918-922, apparently intended for express goods traffic. When new, all except No 921 at Edinburgh were shedded at Balornock, whence they worked to Carlisle (as did No 921) and to Aberdeen. Many of their duties were nocturnal and photographs of them, particularly in action, are rare. A colour plate of 918 was featured in the *Railway Magazine* for March 1907.

Despite weight restrictions and the fact they had longer tenders, three '918s', Nos 918, 920 and 921, were drafted to Oban shed in the summer of 1914 to assist with the heavy tourist traffic. This at times presented the interesting spectacle of a large-boilered and small-boilered version of what was mechanically the same engine double-heading a heavy train. Two years later Nos 918 and 919 received heavy repairs in Darlington at the works of Robert Stephenson & Co, who repainted them a very dark shade of blue, possibly similar to that applied by Hawthorn Leslie & Co to the 'Rivers' and five years later by Armstrong Whitworth & Co (also on Tyneside) to ten new Pickersgill 4-4-0s.

One wonders whether in practice these big-boilered, small-wheeled 4-6-0s were ever justified, as their work could surely have been carried out more competently and with greater efficiency by a McIntosh standard '812' 0-6-0, of which cylinders, driving wheel diameter, adhesion weight and effective boiler capacity were very similar. Like the lumbering '600' 0-8-0s, the '918' 4-6-0s were by 1922 virtually white elephants with a probable life expectancy of only a few more years, regardless of the ensuing and ruthless LMS locomotive standardisation programme under which other more effective McIntosh units continued to flourish.

Immediately after the '918' class St Rollox turned out ten rather similar engines, CR Nos 908-917, in which the driving wheel diameter was increased to 5ft 9in. As in the '903' and '918' class, the coupling rods incorporated a knuckle joint in order to facilitate ½in side play in the trailing coupled axle. In recent years the '908' series have often been referred to as mixed-traffic engines, but contemporary documents make it quite clear that they were regarded as passenger engines when built and they were so employed for about 10 years. Four engines, Nos 909, 911, 912 and 914, worked the Clyde boat trains between Glasgow Central and Gourock. The first two were actually named (see Chapter 12) and were shedded at Greenock, the other two being at Polmadie. Driving wheels of 5ft 9in diameter were long associated with the Clyde Coast workings, from the Drummond 4-4-0 'Coast Bogies' of 1888-1891, through the 908s to the Pickersgill 4-6-2Ts of 1917, which in turn were superseded by the various LMS standard 2-6-4T classes. The remaining '908' engines were largely divided between Balornock and Perth (Nos 908, 913 and 917) to handle the Glasgow-Perth-Aberdeen passenger service , including the 'Grampian'. Surviving records do not suggest that they were in any way outstanding performers. At some stage in its career No 917 featured in the Clyde Coast workings, but in 1910 it was moved from Perth to Edinburgh to work vacuum-fitted freights to Carlisle. Like Nos 918 and 919, the 5ft 9in 4-6-0s Nos 908, 909, 912, 916 and 917 were equipped with vacuum ejectors.

During World War I the '908' class relinquished their various passenger duties and became goods engines. Allocations were rationalised as follows: Nos 908-912 to Balornock, Nos 913-914 to Perth and Nos 915-917 to Edinburgh. The Balornock quintet worked express goods trains to Aberdeen, Carlisle and to Stirling and Grangemouth. The '908' and '918' boilers were very similar, except that the former had tubes some 17in longer (15ft) and both were particularly badly proportioned. The small fireboxes would have promoted high and uneconomic combustion rates. Whilst often a highly desirable feature the unusually generous free gas area (which amounted to almost 20 per cent of the grate area in these boilers) meant that when working hard much of the small coal and fines must have been lifted clean off the shallow grate and blasted through the chimney long before combustion was complete. Ashpan design was also poor and so firing these two classes, unlike the more prolific 4-4-0s and 0-6-0s, was not only an extremely arduous task but also one demanding great skill. It is thus not surprising that in late CR days both the '908' and '918' classes in freight service consumed a collosal 90-100lb of coal to the mile! It was regrettable that a proposal to superheat the '908' engines failed to mature, meaning another twenty years of backache for the unfortunate firemen concerned.

A curious little mystery concerns engine No 917, which was initially at Perth and which as the last survivor also ended its days there. The *Locomotive* for February 1907 stated that 'The last of this series, No 917, is now running, and it differs from the rest in having a new pattern of cab, with two windows on each side-sheet and the roof overhanging at the back.' This is remarkably prophetic as the official record states that the engine was so altered in 1910, when it was illustrated in the technical press including *The Locomotive* for January 1910. The latter was so early in the year in question that one suspects that the engine was indeed built new with this feature, which for some reason was not illustrated for three years, and that the official record was mistakenly amended in retrospect on this account. The cab itself was reminiscent of those provided by William Pickersgill on the Great North of Scotland Railway (but not repeated when he later moved to the Caledonian) and those of the North British Atlantics. Although it would have featured on McIntosh's proposed Pacific, it was only repeated in 11 new superheated 4-6-0s which constituted his last new locomotive design before his retirement in 1914.

These engines, which were effectively superheated versions of the '908' class, were easily McIntosh's best 4-6-0s, but they could have been even better had they been provided with larger fireboxes instead of retaining the quite inadequate 21sq ft grate of the earlier engines. Built in two batches, they were quite definitely intended as express goods engines and they rarely featured on passenger workings in CR days, although in 1914 it was reported that No 179 was regularly working the 'Grampian' out of Buchanan Street.

Three engines, Nos 179, 188 and 189, were at Carlisle and worked night goods to Perth and Dundee until early LMS days. Four similar engines, Nos 184-187, were at Perth, three of which worked alternately with the Carlisle engines on the Carlisle and Dundee night workings. The remaining engine worked by day to Aberdeen, which had no 4-6-0 allocation and instead used a 4-4-0 in alternation. The remainder, Nos 180-183, were at Balornock, where two alternately ran the midday goods to Aberdeen, which was known for many years as the 'Jubilee'. The other pair similarly handled another regular Aberdeen turn on which they were later joined by two '908s', No 908 itself and No 912, to alternate on a turn to Carlisle. These two latter '908' engines are both believed to have been repaired in England during 1916-1920, when St Rollox was hard-pressed. In fact, No 908 languished for about 18 months from August 1918 at the works of the Yorkshire Engine Co, whose surviving records indicate that no fewer than eleven Scottish 4-6-0s were repaired there between 1916 and 1920; these were Caledonian Nos 908 and 918-921, and Highland Nos 106, 107, 109, 115, 116, and 'Castle' 141.

Compared to a voracious '908', a newly outshopped '179' could show a tremendous fuel economy operating on as little, relatively speaking, as 48lb to the mile. However, over the course of about 18 months, owing to wear of the single broad piston valve rings, consumption could steadily rise to over 70lb per mile.

A '179' weighed 4½ tons more than a '908', a fact not simply accounted for by the superheater, which was of the Robinson pattern that had by now been

48

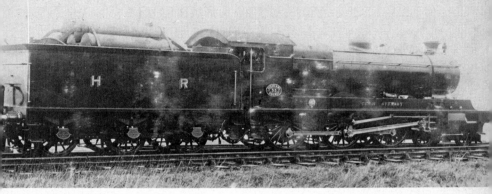

HR 'Clan' 4–6–0s

Top: HR No 55 *Clan Mackinnon* new at Perth in 1921./*H. Gordon Tidey*

Above: Clan Stewart equipped as an oil burner in 1921./*LPC*

Below: Clan Chattan heads a northbound express near Perth. Note the smokebox decorations./*Rixon Bucknall Collection*

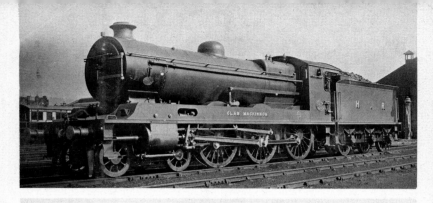

Top: Clan Mackinnon in HR green./Ian Allan Library

Above: An immaculate Clan Chattan in early LMS red livery. Note removal of cylinder tail rods./Ian Allan Library

Below: Westinghouse-fitted Clan Fraser at speed near Luncarty./H. Gordon Tidey

Above right: Clan Munro leaves Dalnaspidal station to make the final onslaught on Drumochter Summit./Ian Allan Library

Right: Clan Mackinnon prepares to leave Kyle of Lochalsh with a cattle train in September 1948./C. C. Herbert

Top: A 'Clan' fitted with a CR-type chimney marshalls a goods train. */Ian Allan Library*

Above: The last survivor, *Clan Mackinnon* at Inverness in June 1949. */H. C. Casserley*

McIntosh 6ft 6in 4-6-0s

Top right: A rare view of CR No 49 on trial at Dundee when brand-new. The tender has been detached in order to enable the engine to be turned./*LPC*

Centre right: The second McIntosh 6ft 6in 4-6-0 No 50 *Sir James Thompson* when new in blue livery. Note the large tender initials./*Real Photographs*

Bottom right: A close up study of the same engine./*Rixon Bucknall Collection*

Top: CR No 903 brand-new in lined shop grey as yet un-named./*LPC*

Above: CR No 903 in blue livery and named *Cardean*./*LPC*

Below: Another study of No 903 showing the elegant reversing rod.
/*Rixon Bucknall Collection*

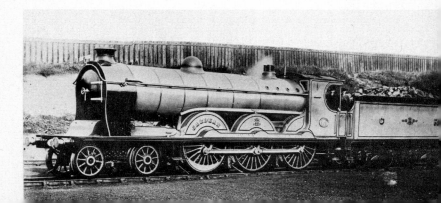

Top: Cardean heads the 'Up Corridor' out of Glasgow Central, the engine's regular duty for ten years./Rixon Bucknall Collection

Above: No 907 newly rebuilt with superheater and piston valves./LPC

Below: A broadside study of No 906 as similarly rebuilt. Note superheater damper gear on smokebox side and mechanical lubricator on footplate. The cabs of these engines were modified by Pickersgill in line with those of his own 4-6-0s, as seen here./Rixon Bucknall Collection

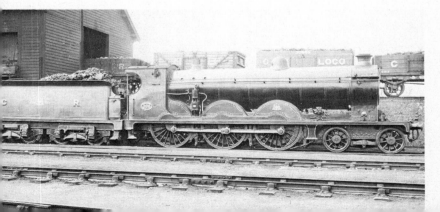

Top left: A rather battered *Cardean* after the Crawford accident of April 1909. /*Crown Copyright, National Railway Museum, York*

Centre left: In superheated form No 906 hauls the Up Glasgow Diner through Rockcliffe./*Rixon Bucknall Collection*

Bottom left: The ill-fated No 907 in final condition approaches Beattock Summit with a southbound express./*H. Gordon Tidey*

Below: The two 1903 McIntosh 4-6-0s ended their days working between Perth and Aberdeen. No 14750 (ex-CR No 49) is seen leaving Perth with an express for the Granite City./*LPC*

Bottom: In LMS black livery and devoid of smokebox wingplates, No 14750 at Perth in 1933 shortly before withdrawal./*C. C. B. Herbert*

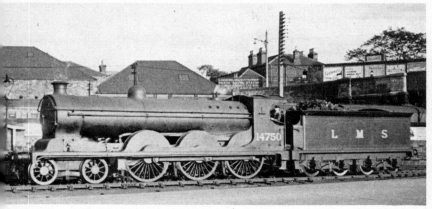

Above: The two Perth-based 'Cardeans' as Nos 14753 and 14754 double-head an express for the south out of Aberdeen in early LMS days. The pilot engine has 'pop' safety valves and a large non-standard Westinghouse pump fitted by Pickersgill. */Ian Allan Library*

Below: CR No 906 as LMS No 14755 in red livery. The engine retains its superheater damper gear. Unlike the two 1903 engines the 1906 passenger 4-6-0s retained their smokebox wingplates to the end./*Ian Allan Library*

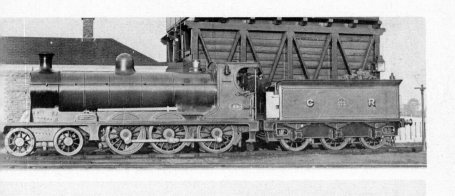

McIntosh 5ft and 5ft 9in 4-6-0s

Top: CR No 59 illustrates the simple elegance of McIntosh's special 'Oban' 4-6-0./*Ian Allan Library*

Above: The first McIntosh 4-6-0 No 55, in plain shop grey whilst undergoing trials. /*Rixon Bucknall Collection*

Below: One of the 1905-built 'Oban Bogies' officially posed near St Rollox at the head of a rake of brand-new 12-wheeled Edinburgh-Glasgow stock./*LPC*

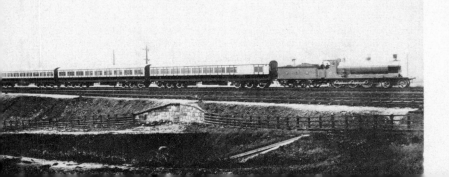

Top left: With MacCaig's Tower in the background McIntosh 5ft 4-6-0 No 52 storms away from Oban with a Midland carriage next to the tender. */Rixon Bucknall Collection*

Centre left: Official portrait of McIntosh 'Express Goods' 4-6-0 No 918./*LPC*

Bottom left: No 919 on shed. Running along the footplate can be seen the 'through pipe' permitting the working of vacuum-fitted freight trains. No 918 and several of the '908' class were similarly equipped./*Rixon Bucknall Collection*

Above: A graphic illustration of the prodigous appetite for coal of the McIntosh '918' class. In this official CR photograph the smokebox of No 921 is half-filled with ash./*Crown Copyright, National Railway Museum, York*

Top: An unidentified '918' engine heads a freight through Stirling./*R. A. Chrystal*

Above: No 920, its smokebox wingplates removed by Pickersgill, powers a freight train which includes an 0-4-0 industrial tank engine (probably ex-Andrew Barclay & Co) next to the tender./*Rixon Bucknall Collection*

Top right: McIntosh 5ft 9in mixed-traffic 4-6-0 No 908 in mint condition./*LPC*

Centre right: The last '908' engine, No 917, with side-window cab. /*Rixon Bucknall Collection*

Bottom right: McIntosh superheated 5ft 9in express goods 4-6-0 No 189./*LPC*

Top: No 914 at Glasgow Central with a Gourock train./*Rixon Bucknall Collection*

Above: No 917 at Glasgow Central also displays the Clyde coast semaphore code.
/*Rixon Bucknall Collection*

adopted as standard on the CR. These superheater 4-6-0s were very strongly built and featured a return to the $1\frac{1}{8}$in thick frames of Nos 49 and 50. The engines were given 9in trick-ported piston valves above the cylinders in place of the slide valves hitherto located between. This enabled a reduction of 3in to be made from the standard 2ft $4\frac{1}{2}$in centre-to-centre spacing, thus actually anticipating Pickersgill's subsequent practice, and allowing the provision of $9\frac{1}{2}$in by 9in driving axleboxes. If only McIntosh had given these engines 6ft coupled wheels and a shortened '903' boiler he would have produced a really useful and reasonably efficient general purpose engine.

There was a large measure of interchangeability of major components between McIntosh's various 4-4-0 and 0-6-0 classes, and his 0-4-4 and 0-6-0 tank engines, but the spares position regarding the various 4-6-0 classes would appear to have been a nightmare. In practice the situation was not so bad. The cylinder blocks of the '55', '908' and '918' classes were standard with those of the 4-4-0 classes, but the boilers might have caused difficulties. However, although each 4-6-0 class had its own design of boiler it was not St Rollox practice to maintain a stock of spare boilers in any case; each engine retained the same boiler with which it was built from one heavy repair to the next (which took place about every two years, and lasted about two months) and throughout its life. (There is some evidence, however, that a *third* boiler was built for use on Nos 49 and 50). As to the boilers themselves, the diameters of the '903', '908', '918' and '179' classes were the same, and the throatplates and backplates all utilised the same flanging blocks. The three 1906-built classes all had smokebox and firebox tubeplates drilled to the same pattern and those of the '179' class were similarly interchangeable with the '903' engines in their superheated form. The fireboxes of the '908', '918' and '179' classes were identical, and there was some standardisation of tube lengths.

No replacement boilers were later built for the McIntosh 4-6-0s, which is why two 'Oban' 4-6-0s, ex-CR Nos 52 and 53, were later rebuilt in 1930 with boilers off withdrawn '918' class engines Nos 922 and 919, respectively. These rebuilds also acquired the wider cab but retained their short wheelbase tenders. So modified, former CR No 52 as LMS No 14606 ran until November 1937 as the last survivor, and could be seen pottering about at Oban to the end. The original CR No 55 was withdrawn in September 1934 having covered 1,033,209 miles, whilst the longest-lived was the last of the 1902 batch, No 59, which when retired late in December 1936 had covered 1,147,677 miles. The 'Oban' 4-6-0s were thus genuinely worn out when scrapped.

Latterly the McIntosh 4-6-0s were but a shadow of their former glory, painted black, and shorn of their smokebox wingplates, which process had actually begun before 1923. The last representatives of this rare but handsome breed were two of the superheated '179' class, ex-179 itself and No 182, which were reprieved by the Second World War but scrapped soon after it had ended.

The penchant around the turn of the century of the Belgian State Railways for inside-cylinder engines of basically McIntosh Caledonian Railway design is fairly well known. Following the purchase from Neilson Reid & Co in 1898 of five 'Dunalastair II-type 4-4-0s, several hundred 4-4-0s and 0-6-0s were subsequently built in Belgium itself over the next few years; one of the latter was observed by the author at Ostend as recently as 1965. There was also a similar 4-4-2T with no direct CR equivalent, but probably more obscure were 42 inside-cylinder 4-6-0s of Type 35 constructed by no fewer than five Belgian builders between 1903 and 1905. These bore an obvious resemblance to McIntosh's 'Oban' 4-6-0, but appearances were deceptive. The engines weighed around 70 tons and had 5ft 3in diameter boilers pitched 8½ft above rail, but because the generous Continental loading gauge allowed a maximum height of 14ft the relative proportions looked much the same.

The statistics of these Belgian 4-6-0s are somewhat complex. The earlier engines had equally spaced 5ft 3in diameter coupled wheels, but there was an increase to 5ft 7in diameter in later machines. Many of the later engines also ranked amongst the earliest European locomotives to have (Schmidt) superheaters and actually weighed slightly less than their saturated predecessors. All the engines had $1^5/_{16}$in thick main frames, 20½in by 26in piston valve cylinders, and 199lb pressure boilers. In order to burn the *briquettes* traditional in Belgium, a long 30½sq ft grate was provided, but it is interesting to note that the curious McIntosh practice of deliberately offsetting the blastpipe with respect to the chimney was adhered to at least in the saturated engines, where the discrepancy was no less than one inch!

These engines were extensively employed in heavy passenger and goods traffic operating at only moderate speeds in the hilly Luxembourg region. Several disappeared during the course of World War I, after which the picture was highly confused. Some formerly superheated engines were running with saturated boilers and *vice versa*, and similarly engines formerly having 5ft 3in wheels got the larger wheels: and so on. The surviving engines are said to have been 'modernised' during the 1920s, but all had gone by the end of 1929.

It appears generally to have been assumed that, whereas McIntosh strongly influenced Belgian practice for a time, there was no reciprocal effect on St Rollox thinking. It is pure conjecture on the author's part this might not be

Historical Summary of the McIntosh 4-6-0 Classes

Class	CR Nos	Built	St Rollox Order No	LMS Nos	Withdrawn
49	49, 50	3-4/1903	Y69	14750-1	1933
55	55-59	5-6/1902	Y66	14600-4	1928-1937
	51-54	8-9/1905	Y75	14605-8	
179	179-183	1913	Y107	17905-9	1935-1946
	184-189	1914	Y112	17910-15	
903	903-907	5-7/1906	Y80	14752-5*	(1916) 1927-1930
908	908-917	10-12/1906	Y81	14609-18	1930-1935
918	918-922	7-9/1906	Y79	17900-4	1929-1930

* No 907 was scrapped in 1916 as a result of the Quintinshill Disaster and so never carried an LMS number.

strictly true. It may be that the later 5ft 7in Belgian 4-6-0s inspired McIntosh to build the '908' 4-6-0s for the Caledonian Railway. On a more superficial level the side-window cab on the final example of these engines might have been inspired by the pattern fitted to the Belgian 4-6-0s (some of the 'Belgianised' 4-4-0s had three side windows). One constructional feature of the Belgian engines that was certainly used in the later McIntosh 4-6-0s was the tri-partite outer firebox, with direct stays screwed into the thicker centre plate. This type of construction, whilst not unique, was unusual. It is quite possible that the Belgians sent McIntosh drawings of what they had developed from his basic designs, but such data could also have been gleaned by St Rollox from the technical press of that time.

CHAPTER SEVEN

The Pickersgill '60' Class

J. F. McIntosh's locomotives were noted for their robust construction, but they were put in the shade on this score by the engines built by his successor, William Pickersgill. In contrast to the flamboyant McIntosh, Pickersgill was a reserved Englishman who nevertheless thought big. Whereas McIntosh had never gone beyond 1⅛in thickness for locomotive main frames, Pickersgill built all his 4-4-0s and two larger classes of 4-6-0 on to massively cross-braced frames 1¼in thick. He also provided appreciably more generous bearing surfaces by pitching the inside cylinders closer together in his 4-4-0s and 0-6-0s, and placing the cylinders outside the frames in his 4-6-0s.

In addition to massive physique Pickersgill's locomotives were generally notable for their sluggishness. After the halcyon days of the McIntosh era, Pickersgill was spared potential embarrassment on this account simply because, before he had time to produce any new engines, the outbreak of the First World War brought about an immediate deceleration in schedules, which never fully recovered before 1923. The resultant lower speeds were reflected in six new passenger 4-6-0s, authorised early in 1915 at a total estimated cost of £15,750, which were to have a driving wheel diameter of 6ft 1in. This rather curious dimension had long been a standard on Pickersgill's previous line, the Great North of Scotland, of which he had been Locomotive Superintendent for no fewer than 20 years.

Such were the wartime pressures on St Rollox that some other new construction, and even some locomotive repairs, had to be let to outside contractors. Not until November 1916 was the first of the new 4-6-0s, No 60, completed. It was remarkable in being the first main-line locomotive with outside cylinders to be built for the Caledonian Railway since the original 'Oban Bogies' of 1882. Its outside cylinders and larger bearings made the engine a more serviceable proposition in wartime than the big inside-cylinder McIntosh 4-6-0s. In other respects, however, it is not generally appreciated that the boiler of Pickersgill's first 4-6-0 was almost a duplicate of that of the superheated 903 class, but chopped back to only three rings in the barrel. In place of the Schmidt installation of the McIntosh machines the Pickersgill engine was fitted with the Robinson superheater. The latter's short loop elements provided exactly half the heating surface of its Schmidt counterpart, although this did not necessarily point to low degree superheat. Nevertheless, Pickersgill's attitude to superheating in general does not appear to have been one of enthusiasm, rather that it was a contemporary evil to be avoided altogether if at all possible.

Although the Caledonian, like the other Scottish companies, never made use of water troughs, Pickersgill discontinued the practice of building large bogie tenders. The tender of his new 4-6-0 was standard with those of his 4-4-0s.

By the end of April 1917 all six engines were in traffic. No 60 itself, distinguished by Ross 'pop' safety valves, was stationed at Balornock and worked principally to Dundee. No 61 was sent to Polmadie, where David Gibson, no doubt regretfully, forsook *Cardean* to work 'the Corridor' with this new charge. Nos 62 and 63 at Carlisle handled the Carlisle-Glasgow and Carlisle-Edinburgh services. Predictably perhaps, Nos 64 and 65 were at Perth, where they took over less successfully the duties of the two 'Rivers' between Glasgow and Aberdeen. In practice the Pickersgill '60' class supplemented rather than superseded the older McIntosh 4-6-0s, which in speed could still show the new arrivals a clean pair of heels at any time.

A '60' probably never exceeded 65mph in CR days. The legendary lethargy of this design has been attributed to the Stephenson valve gear. In the past this has sometimes wrongly been stated to have been of the 'crossed-rod' variety, which would give decreasing lead as the engine was notched up, to the detriment of its performance. In fact the gear was simply of the direct connected inside admission type, operating 9in trick-ported piston valves, and was very similar to that of Pickersgill's contemporary 4-6-2 tank engines. The latter, with 5ft 9in driving wheels, had identical cylinders and were comparatively lively performers. This leads one to suppose that the trouble with the 4-6-0s was merely one of valve setting, which should have been easy to rectify. However, no one ever seems to have taken the trouble to experiment, even when 20 further engines, slightly modified in other respects, came to be built a few years later. On test south of Carlisle the first of the latter was uncharacteristically coaxed up to 73mph downhill, at which speed the hammerblow must have been about 10 tons! (See Appendix).

A Pickersgill '60' 4-6-0 was not a sophisticated engine, just a straightforward job. Indeed, a small sectional drawing of one has been used in a well known encyclopaedia for many years to illustrate the rudiments of a steam locomotive. It steamed well, rode well, pulled reasonably hard, and was rarely known to slip. Despite its medium-sized driving wheels its factor of adhesion was unusually high at almost 6. This low power-to-weight ratio was due to liberal construction, particularly the massive diagonally cross-braced 1¼in main frames, which were completely immune to cracks.

Notwithstanding their generous bearing surfaces (9½in by 11in on the coupled axles) the Pickersgill 4-6-0s suffered from heating troubles because lubrication was never a strong point at St Rollox. The '60' class ran on average about 160,000 miles between general repairs and 130,000 miles between boiler changes. Unlike the other CR 4-6-0 classes, each individual engine of which religiously retained the self-same boiler through thick and thin, the boilers on the 26 members of the '60' class circulated quite freely from engine to engine in LMS days. In addition, several boilers were built for the class at St Rollox between 1928 and 1943.

After grouping the former Caledonian had a rather unexpected 'posthumous' last fling when 20 more '60' 4-6-0s were built at St Rollox during 1925-26. In these cylinder diameter was slightly increased, tail rods were omitted, and a new pattern of bogie with independent suspension for each axle was fitted. The tenders were smaller and in many cases were provided with water pick-up apparatus in anticipation of the completion of new water troughs at Strawfank and Gretna. Many of this batch when new were stationed at Carlisle (Kingmoor) and there were thoughts of using them on fast freights south over Shap. For a short period examples did sometimes appear in the Liverpool and Manchester areas, but the introduction of the LMS standard 'Crab' 2-6-0 quickly reinstated Carlisle as their most southerly limit of working.

An official photograph of 64 in red livery as LMS 14654 shows the engine carrying a 'Cardean' pattern chimney. By all accounts this was afterwards carried for three years (1925-1928) by the pioneer '60' itself as LMS 14650, and possibly finished up on one of the LMS-built engines. In fact the *standard* Pickersgill chimney was almost identical in profile with those of the larger McIntosh 4-6-0s but was plain in form and cast in one piece. On the subject of chimneys, those of Pickersgill's smaller 'Oban' 4-6-0s anticipated in style the chimneys of the early Stanier LMS locomotives to a remarkable degree, although E. S. Cox has remarked that the latter were derived from the McIntosh pattern.

It is remarkable that when the original CR batch were turned out St Rollox had found the time and resources to adorn the engines in the glory of the traditional blue livery fully lined out and quite undiminished in any way. (Certain other British railways which had been noted for their elaborate locomotive liveries abandoned these for ever in favour of plain grey after 1914). Following a brief interlude in red, black was the order of the day for the 'Sixties' from 1928. It could well have been their long and usually grimy boilers that prompted the nickname of 'Greybacks' for these engines in later years. Alternatively it has been suggested that this term, also the Scots expression for a 'louse', was disparagingly applied by South Western men when the 4-6-0s began to work regularly over the former G&SWR lines in the 1930s. It was hardly to be expected that praise would be lavished upon a product of St Rollox, and indeed the engines made a poor showing over the hilly Girvan road. Nevertheless, they were not totally incapable of putting up a brisk performance, even over an 'alien' road, for in 1939 David L. Smith recorded 14633 hauling 340 tons full over the undemanding 33·7 miles from Ayr to Paisley at an average speed of 57·2mph, and he noted a maximum of 68mph by a '60' over this stretch.

After the war most of the class were concentrated at Hamilton and Motherwell sheds. An interesting development shortly after Nationalisation was the allocation of a few survivors to the former NBR shed at St Margarets in

CR No	St Rollox Order	Date built	LMS No	Withdrawn
60	Y115	1916	14650	1953
61-65	Y116	1916-17	14651-55	1944-52
—	(Y131)	1925-26	14630-49	1946-53

Edinburgh. It is not known whether one from thence ever traversed the Waverley Route, which was never strongly associated with the 4-6-0 type, but survivors could still be seen at Carlisle as late as 1952. The former No 60 itself was the longest-lived and as BR No 54650 was withdrawn in September 1953, whilst the last survivor, which was also the last Scottish 4-6-0 to remain in service, was retired three months later as BR No 54639.

McIntosh had built eight powerful 0-8-0s during 1901-1903, but thereafter the 0-6-0 remained the standard freight engine on the Caledonian. A 2-8-0 version of Pickersgill's '60' 4-6-0 would have been an interesting and doubtless long-lived proposition. All other things being equal, the two major defects of the passenger design, ie its valve setting and rather small grate, would not have been so apparent in a goods engine. As far as the author is aware no such proposal was ever made, but in 1917 a brutish 2-6-0 heavy freight engine was designed in some detail, in much the same mould as the '60' class. Why the driving wheel diameter was to have been 5ft 8in, when 5ft 9in was a long-established St Rollox standard, is a mystery. Another curious feature was that the superheater would have consisted of single return elements housed in 24 flues of 3¼in diameter. Such an installation would have imparted only a minimal degree of superheat — just one of several indications of Pickersgill's unenthusiastic attitude to superheating.

The general arrangement drawing of this engine, dated July 26, 1917, does not bear Pickersgill's signature. The proposal was shelved largely because the refuge loop capacity between Glasgow and Carlisle could not have accommodated the size of train the engine would have been capable of hauling.

Four years later, however, Pickersgill was very impressed by the work of the new Gresley three-cylinder 5ft 8in 2-6-0s on 600ton GNR passenger trains during the 1921 Coal Strike. The following year St Rollox designed a massive 5ft 6in 2-6-0 having 'River'-type cylinders and a shortened '956' boiler. As has been described by E. S. Cox in *Locomotive Panorama* Vol I (Ian Allan 1965), this was re-vamped by the newly-formed LMSR and eventually emerged in 1926 as the familiar 'Crab' 2-6-0.

CHAPTER EIGHT

St Rollox Swan Song

Whilst Gresley's big 2-6-0s were hauling their prodigous loads out of Kings Cross, St Rollox was completing four very large 4-6-0s which displayed several remarkable similarities. When compared to the Doncaster engine, the new Caledonian 4-6-0 had the same cylinder dimensions, boiler pressure, grate area, and 20ton axleload. Appearance was not dissimilar, for both locomotives had a particularly large round-topped boiler surmounted by a squat chimney, but more than anything else both designs incorporated three-cylinder propulsion and a derived valve gear to operate the inside piston valve.

Other than giving an initial lead in 1908-9 with four large 0-8-4 shunting tanks and a converted 4-4-2 passenger engine, the Great Central Railway had not taken three-cylinder propulsion any further. For almost a decade the North Eastern had been virtually alone in building quite a number of three-cylinder locomotives for a wide range of duties. But in May 1918 H. N. Gresley on the Great Northern Railway completed a three-cylinder version of his standard two-cylinder 2-8-0 coal engine, employing a highly complicated mechanism connected to the outside valve gear to actuate the inside piston valve.

This idea was by no means new, for in 1909 Herbert Holcroft, a young engineer on the Great Western, had patented a rather simpler mechanism for a three-cylinder locomotive, whilst similar developments were afoot in Germany at the time. Swindon, of course, never built any three-cylinder locomotives, and in 1914 Holcroft moved to the South Eastern & Chatham Railway. Four years later, in November 1918, he read a paper on three-cylinder locomotives to the Institution of Locomotive Engineers which aroused considerable interest. As a result, Holcroft came into contact with Gresley. Somewhat to the chagrin of Holcroft's chief, R. E. L. Maunsell, Holcroft collaborated with Gresley in order to develop the latter's valve gear and a very much improved version subsequently appeared on the prototype GNR large-boilered three-cylinder 2-6-0 No 1000 in March 1920.

Holcroft's original basic valve gear, of which an illustration can be found on p.85 of his book *Locomotive Adventure* (Ian Allan 1962), was effectively utilised in Pickersgill's new Caledonian 4-6-0s, but in an unnecessarily complicated form. As all three cylinders lay in the same horizontal plane, the valve gear could have been used in symmetrical form exactly as Holcroft had originally designed it, but for some peculiar reason best known to St Rollox the valve gear was arranged to operate in the vertical plane, which thereby increased the number of pins from nine to fifteen. Each pin was a potential source of wear, the

56

effects of which would be multiplied many times in a mechanism of this type; that would have made some nonsense of St. Rollox's 'pin allowance' of only ⅛in for valve-setting purposes.

Despite the apparent similarities between GNR 2-6-0 No 1000 and CR 4-6-0 No 956, the fact that the St Rollox general arrangement drawing is dated March 9, 1920, ie precisely one week after the Gresley 2-6-0 was first steamed at Doncaster, strongly suggests that the Scottish engine was the product of original thought. Nevertheless, it is a fact that Gresley and Pickersgill were both prominent members of the wartime Association of Railway Locomotive Engineers Standard Locomotive Committee. This Committee's abortive proposals, of which some details are to be found in *Trains Illustrated* for February 1954, were to have been characterised by unusually large boilers (as were Nos 1000 and 956) and it is probable that committee members were at times given to discussing their individual ideas for post-war development, thereby influencing each other to some degree.

As already mentioned, the boilers of the '956' class were particularly large, having a maximum girth of 5ft 9in and extending 16ft between tubeplates. They cost £2,367 each to produce. The smokebox rested upon a saddle formed by the inside cylinder casting. All three cylinders lay in line abreast, although because the inside cylinder drove on to the leading coupled axle, and the outside pair on to the centre coupled wheels, there was a great disparity in connecting rod lengths, 6ft 6in against 11ft respectively, despite the provision of outside piston rods 6½ft in length. Externally the engines were beautifully proportioned, and finished in lined blue livery and red cylinders must have made a magnificent sight.

Unfortunately here was not a case of 'handsome is as handsome does'. Rather strangely very little reference was made in the technical press at the time to the derived valve gear of these engines, and although drawings of the engine as a whole were published in *The Railway Engineer* for October 1921 little could be deduced from these. In fact, the gear proved to be a disaster. Although not incorporating any exceptionally long levers, as in the well-known Gresley 2-to-1

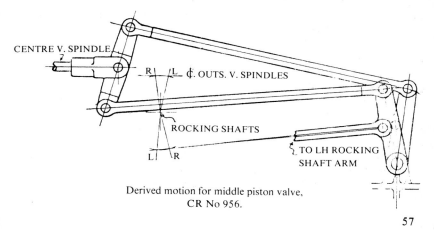

Derived motion for middle piston valve,
CR No 956.

layout, the inside piston valve evidently experienced an unacceptable degree of over-travel, for unsuccessful attempts to check this with dashpot devices were made in No 959 in 1923. Apart from giving poor steam distribution the gear also imposed undue strain on the valve spindle guides; the latter were attached to the slide bars, which were thus caused to fracture. In April 1922, the derived valve gear was removed from Nos 957 and 958, after the engines had only been in traffic for nine months, and was replaced by Stephenson valve gear; Nos 956 and 959 were later similarly altered. The combination of two different valve gears in one locomotive, one with constant, and the other with variable lead, was not a happy union and the sound of a '956' in action has been described as a 'muffled roar'. In addition to these mechanical troubles the boilers were poor steamers.

It is said that when construction of these engines commenced at St. Rollox late in 1920 there was wild speculation as to what the new locomotives were to be, and a Pacific was suggested. It is an interesting fact that, except for an engine allocated to Balornock rather than Polmadie, the distribution of these engines was the same as that envisaged for the four projected McIntosh 4-6-2s of 1913. The pioneer No 956 was shedded hard by main works at Balornock and initially ran in shop grey with an indicator shelter attached — though one shudders to think what manner of diagrams must thus have been obtained. James Grassie, who had latterly driven McIntosh 6ft 6in 4-6-0 No 50, was the regular driver and was about the only man who could get reasonable work out of a Pickersgill three-cylinder 4-6-0. Even he failed lamentably on at least one celebrated occasion, when the engine was experimentally working between Glasgow Central and Carlisle, as we shall see later.

Carlisle Kingmoor received Nos 957 and 958 in July 1921 and the new engines worked alongside Pickersgill 4-6-0s Nos 62 and 63 and McIntosh 4-6-0 No 906. The remaining engine, No 959, went to Perth and worked regularly to Aberdeen. Its regular driver was 'Geordie' Newlands, who previously had driven Pickersgill 4-6-0 No 64 from new, and who prior to that had briefly driven the final 'River' No 943. Were he alive today he could no doubt express some interesting views on the relative merits of latterday Caledonian 4-6-0 classes!

The Pickersgill '956' class was the largest and most powerful passenger locomotive to be inherited by the LMSR in 1923. It was a measure of its utter failure that it did not participate in the ensuing competitive trials of the principal types; the Caledonian contestant was the smaller and earlier '60' design, of which additional engines were actually built. In view of their small numerical strength the LMSR never remotely considered attempting to make any improvements to the three-cylinder engines. As early as 1923 No 957 had a regular goods turn between Edinburgh and Carlisle, alternating with a Midland 0-6-0, and a little later as LMS No 14801 it was frequently to be seen on the former G&SWR main line. By early 1925 all four had been repainted red; No 959 was so treated at Perth Works and was joined at Perth shed by ex-956. The four engines were thereafter divided between two sheds and were largely employed on goods trains. The Carlisle pair lasted rather longer, but all enjoyed only brief existences despite their massive construction.

In 1922 the earliest Caledonian 4-6-0s, those on the Oban line, were 20 years old. Thoughts at St. Rollox turned to their replacement — inevitably, perhaps, to yet another 4-6-0. Orders were placed on the shops for eight engines, but construction had not progressed beyond the fabrication of a few patterns and templates when on May 23 the Board resolved to pass the order on to the North British Locomotive Company simultaneously with a contract for a final twelve Pickersgill 4-4-0s. All 20 engines were to be built at the NBL's Queens Park Works and be delivered between October 25 and December 25, 1922.

An atmosphere of urgency and misfortune appears to have clouded the design and construction of the new 4-6-0s, the first of which, CR No 191, was not delivered until December 12. The remainder emerged at two-three day intervals, with the final engine arriving at St Rollox on December 30, its blue paint scarcely dry when the CR as such ceased to exist. There was no penalty clause in the contract, despite which the makers made a substantial loss on the order on account of raging inflation. Whereas NBL had contracted to build the engines for £5,211 apiece, they actually cost £6,812 each to construct, thus losing the firm nearly £13,000.

Despite the apparent urgency, and the fact that the new 4-6-0s had been designed specifically to operate over the C&O line, they were intially banned on account of restricted platform clearances. Maximum width over cylinders was 8ft 11⅜in; as in all three classes of Pickersgill 4-6-0 (and his 4-6-2T) the outside cylinders were spaced at a rather generous 6ft 9¾in between centres. For the time being six engines remained at St Rollox, and the other two went to Perth, all filling in their time on goods trains. When the ban was lifted Nos 193-5 were sent to Oban shed and the rest were stationed at Stirling and Balmornock before the blue livery disappeared under Derby red and later black paint. During early 1923 these engines appeared as far afield as Aberdeen and Lockerbie on main line goods workings. Incidentally, the Civil Engineer had rejected another 4-6-0 proposal made as early as March 1919 on the ground that it was too heavy for the Oban line. This was for a somewhat larger and more powerful version of the '191' class as later built, estimated to weigh 68½ tons; it would have had 20½in cylinders and the same combination of saturated steam, slide valves and Walschaerts valve gear.

The Pickersgill '191' class was an oddity and looked like some fully-grown version of a freelance essay straight from the pages of the *Model Engineer*. Quite inexplicable at so late a date was the omission of a superheater, and the provision of balanced slide valves actuated by outside Walschaerts valve gear. Steam lap was 1¼in and maximum travel in full gear 5½in, compared to the 1⅛in, and 5⅞in. of the 8in piston valves of a '956'. Pickersgill had a rather in-

CR No*	Date of traffic	LMS No	Date scrapped	Mileage at withdrawal
956	24/6/1921	14800	8/1931	Not known
957	9/7/1921	14801	24/3/1934	281,252
958	8/7/1921	14802	26/1/1935	281,589
959	13/8/1921	14803	4/3/1931	275,893

* St Rollox Order Y125, authorised December 1918, cost per engine £9,665

different attitude to superheating, having built during 1918-1920 the last major class of British saturated steam 0-6-0, and perhaps considered superheating to be unjustified in an engine which would scarcely venture out on the main line proper.

One suggestion has been that the superheater was omitted in order to speed up design work, as the boiler was very similar to that of the 1905 series of McIntosh 'Oban Bogie' with recessed front tube plate, the firebox being increased in length by 7in. However, if it was a question of working in existing components, Pickersgill would have done much better to have used his superheated 4-6-2T boiler, shortened in the boiler barrel by 1ft. The 'Wemyss Bay' tanks were the most spirited performers of any of Pickersgill's designs (which was not saying a great deal). Their cylinders, cast to the same patterns as those of the '60' class 4-6-0s, could also have been utilised. The resultant smaller-wheeled tender version of the 4-6-2T, in effect a 'mini-60', would probably have been a much livelier proposition than that which actually appeared, and which little more than marked time between the demise of the McIntosh 'Oban Bogies' and the advent of the Highland 'Clan' and Stanier Class 5.

Inevitably the new Pickersgills also became known as 'Oban Bogies', although McIntosh's 4-6-0s were still in command and even one or two of the old Brittain 4-4-0s could be seen simmering at Oban. The latter had only four-wheeled tenders, whilst the '191' class was paired with a similar pattern of short wheelbase, six-wheeled tender designed specially for the '55s'. Like the corresponding McIntosh machines, the new Pickersgill 4-6-0s with their very similar boilers, and hence shallow fireboxes, required skilful firing in order to get satisfactory results. Not every fireman was prepared to make the effort and so the engines had a reputation for being shy of steam, but they were by no means universally unpopular. As with the larger '956' class, massive construction did not necessarily confer immunity to mechanical failure. A particular vicissitude of the '191' class was fracture of the slide valve spindle guides behind the cylinders.

In the engines' favour they are reputed to have been very comfortable to ride. This would have been due to the exceptionally high proportion of reciprocating balance incorporated. On the other side of the coin this inflicted excessive hammerblow on the track. Whereas the Report of the Bridge Stress Committee noted the exceptionally low hammerblow values of the 'River' class, it also singled out Pickersgill's '60' and '191' classes, and his 4-6-2T, as having correspondingly very high values. Indeed, the '191' class had the highest total locomotive hammerblow of any of the 120-odd LMS LNER, GWR, and SR tender classes listed (See Appendix). Although Scottish designs predominated amongst the LMSR contribution, unfortunately no determinations were apparently made on Pickersgill's large three-cylinder 4-6-0s, the balance weights of which were equally as large as those of a two-cylinder '60', if not identical.

The '191' class was limited to 230 tons unpiloted over the C&O route. The ex-Highland 'Clans' transferred to the C&O in 1934, which actually weighed ½ton less, showed what could be achieved within a limited weight budget, for they could take on 300tons unassisted. This was largely due to the benefit of a well-proportioned superheated boiler, albeit somewhat small in relation to the large piston valve cylinders. It is interesting to note that Stanier originally proposed to build in 1934-5 a total of 21 63¾ton light 4-6-0s intended specifically for service in Scotland. A diagram of this proposal is illustrated on p.116 of the first of E. S. Cox's admirable books, *Locomotive Panorama* Vol 1, which shows an engine of very similar proportions to the '191' class. These engines were never built, mainly because the Civil Engineer was shortly afterwards prepared to accept its big brother, the Stanier Class 5 4-6-0, over those lines, particularly the C&O, for which the light 4-6-0 had been primarily intended. The fact that the Class 5 did successfully take over the duties of all the remaining Scottish 4-6-0 classes is an oversimplification and does not necessarily indicate excessive duplication of effort in the past. Prior to 1923 no single design of 4-6-0 could have posed as an acceptable replacement for *all* the preceding 4-6-0 classes of either the Highland or Caledonian companies, or both, mainly on account of the weight aspect. The nearest approach to this ideal was, of course, the 'River' class, whose designer suffered for this very reason!

CR No	Makers No*	Delivery date	LMS No	Date scrapped	Mileage at withdrawal
191	22955	12/12/1922	14619	2/11/1940	498,994
192	22956	15/12/1922	14620	30/10/1943	496,553
193	22957	18/12/1922	14621	1/12/1945	530,030
194	22958	20/12/1922	14622	27/11/1943	581,674
195	22959	22/12/1922	14623	30/12/1939	491,662
196	22960	25/12/1922	14624	24/ 2/1940	484,000
197	22961	26/12/1922	14625	25/ 2/1939	501,445
198	22962	30/12/1922	14626	17/ 4/1943	564,131

*NBL Queens Park Order L769, originally allocated St. Rollox Order Y128/9.

Early in 1933, whilst outlining his proposed future new standard locomotive designs, Stanier had initially envisaged applying standardised taper boilers to more than 3,500 existing locomotives. These were to be drawn mainly from the numerically large classes of Derby and Crewe origin, ranging from Class 2F 0-6-0Ts to 'Claughtons'. Rather surprisingly 63 Scottish 4-6-0s were also earmarked, the only engines from north of the Border to be included in this provisional scheme. All four classes of 4-6-0 inherited from the Highland Railway had been selected, along with both varities of ex-Caledonian 'Oban Bogie' 4-6-0. Withdrawal of certain of the non-superheated classes had already begun and the mind boggles at the thought of the venerable frames of Jones 'Big Goods' and McIntosh 'Oban Bogies' carrying tapered Belpaire boilers! (One or two comparable monstrosities had been compounded on the GWR, from whence Stanier had come.) Surprising omissions were the 'Rivers', whose original boilers were beginning to wear out, and the Pickersgill '60' class, whose numerical strength coupled with its robust chassis and low thermal efficiency made it an eminent candidate for renewal with a modern boiler.

In the event, after close investigation this grandiose Stanier boiler replacement scheme was never proceeded with because of the high cost of the detailed alterations which would have been required to the cabs, pipework and frames etc of the recipients, in order to accommodate the new boilers. There would also have been problems associated with modified weight distribution, and whereas at this early stage Stanier was still thinking in terms of low degree superheat, Swindon-style, the supply of superheated steam to elderly slide valve cylinders could have produced some headaches with lubrication.

As regards the Scottish 4-6-0 proposals no diagrams were even prepared, but maximum boiler diameter was envisaged as being 5ft 3in in all cases. The 'Castles' and 'Clans' were to have had a boiler similar to that of the Stanier 2-6-4Ts, but somewhat lengthened in the barrel, grate area being 25sq ft. The other engines were to have received rather smaller boilers with 21¾sq ft grates and so likewise would have shown no advance over the original designs in this respect.

CHAPTER NINE

Caledonian 4-6-0 Performance

A 4-6-0 on a passenger train was a statistical rarity on the Caledonian Railway. By the end of 1922, disregarding the specialist Oban classes, 4-6-0s engaged in passenger service were outnumbered by 4-4-0s in a ratio of about eight to one. In performance the big six-coupled engines nowhere near developed, size for size, the output of their excellent four-coupled brethren, except possibly on very rare occasions, and the Pickersgill 4-6-0s scarcely even equalled the larger 4-4-0s. During the war years 4-4-0s and 4-6-0s alike were indiscriminately loaded up to 450 tons unassisted between Glasgow and Carlisle, and no fewer than 32 new 4-4-0s were added to stock as late as 1920-1922.

Charles Rous-Marten was a personal friend of J. F. McIntosh and wasted no time in getting north to witness at first hand the exploits of Nos 49 and 50 during the notoriously wet summer of 1903. According to the *Railway Magazine* for August 1903 he first glimpsed the great blue bulk of *Sir James Thompson* backing on to his train at Carlisle before the gaze of an admiring throng, held in check by a policeman. With a load of 330 tons, a good start was made from Carlisle and speed fell from 65mph to 50mph over the 8mile 1 in 200 Gretna bank. Beattock, 39¾ miles out, was passed in 43min 10sec, and the ensuing gruelling 10 miles to Summit occupied 23min with a minimum speed of 22mph. Rous-Marten attributed this to a slight disarrangement of the dampers, for he referred in passing to another run with the same engine on an identical load when this exacting stretch was covered in only 19min. He made no reference in either instance to banking assistance, which was optional and often disregarded when Nos 49 and 50 were newly in service.

A more detailed account devoted entirely to these two engines by Rous-Marten, entitled 'The New Caledonian Giants at Work', appeared in *The Engineer* for 21 August 1903. At this time, and for many years afterwards, the 2pm up 'Corridor' was allowed 2hr 15min over the 102½ miles from Glasgow to Carlisle, and No 49 departed south with 390 tons behind the tender. At Carstairs the train was halted for 5min 23sec by adverse signals, but by Thankerton speed had got up to 50mph, only to be checked twice by signals near Symington, leaving 66min for the remaining 63miles to Carlisle. Up the 1 in 150 approaching Elvanfoot speed did not fall below 47.3mph, but had diminished to a sustained 33mph up the final 1 in 100 approach to Summit. (In the *Railway Magazine* account it was alleged that there was possibly a slight acceleration towards the end of this climb).

Commenting on the time of 34min 8sec taken in covering the 23½ miles from

Carstairs to Summit, Rous-Marten exclaimed that 'such a performance with so vast a load on such a gradient has never been equalled in my experience.' The corresponding descent was taken with some caution, but on the home straight to Carlisle over the falling 1 in 200 grade through Gretna, speed rose to a maximum of 79mph and was still 67mph when sweeping through Floriston Woods. Carlisle was reached 29sec under the booked time, and with due allowance for signal slacks and the corresponding acceleration and deceleration involved, net running time from Glasgow to Carlisle was estimated at only 2hr 4min, a very creditable performance over such a difficult road by a new engine with a heavy train.

Rous-Marten returned to Glasgow the same evening behind No 49, which was again hauling 390 tons. Its powers of acceleration were good, for speed was already 60mph when passing Rockcliffe only 4 miles out, and reached 64.2mph before settling down to a minimum of 47mph up the continuous 1 in 200 through Gretna and Kirkpatrick. Unfortunately, owing to a 3min late delivery of the train at Carlisle by the LNWR (with two engines!), the interesting prospect of a single-handed ascent of the Beattock incline was dashed when assistance from a 0-4-4T was accepted. In descending to Strawfank (ie Carstairs) Junction, where the Edinburgh portion was detached, the maximum speed was 75mph. The load was thereafter 280 tons and Glasgow Eglinton Street was reached 2min ahead of the booked time.

With respect to the sister engine, No 50, Rous-Marten timed it with 384 tons to cover the 73½ miles from Carstairs to Carlisle in 78min 14sec. Two signal checks brought the net time down to 76½min.; the final 50 miles from Summit to Carlisle had been covered in 43min 5sec net.

The following year, 1904, saw the introduction of McIntosh's superb large-boilered 'Dunalastair IV' 4-4-0. Rous-Marten recorded in *The Engineer* for 8 December, 1905 an almost unbelievable run behind the pioneer No 140 with Driver Will Stavert. No 140 hauled a train estimated at 404 tons full from Edinburgh Princes Street, piloted as far as Cobbinshaw Summit by a rebuilt Conner 7ft 2-4-0. Blessed with calm dry weather the engine was progressively opened up beyond Strawfank (Carstairs) Junction, but before Lamington running was assisted by short stretches of down grades. However, to quote Rous-Marten's own words, 'up the 10 miles of unbroken ascent, chiefly at 1 in 250, 1 in 200, 1 in 300, between Lamington and Elvanfoot, the speed never fell below 43 miles an hour and the average was 46.5. But the final two miles of 1 in 100 to the Beattock summit constituted the real crux of the whole journey. Here the speed at first dropped steadily, as was certain to be the case with so vast a load on such a grade. In the end it fell to exactly 36 miles an hour, but at this point it kept steadily, quarter mile after quarter mile, until the summit was reached, each quarter-mile being covered in exactly 25seconds . . .'

If one analyses this final climb between Elvanfoot and Summit using the locomotive resistance formula given by E. C. Poultney in *The Locomotive* for June 1944, and the passenger stock resistance formula due to Johansen, one obtains a cylinder horsepower of 1530 and a corresponding calculated drawbar horsepower of 1145. These figures are almost certainly over-estimates, but the

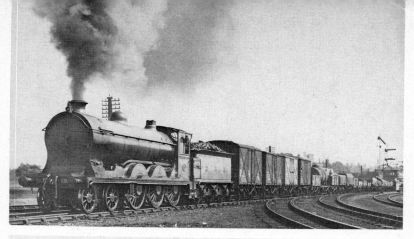

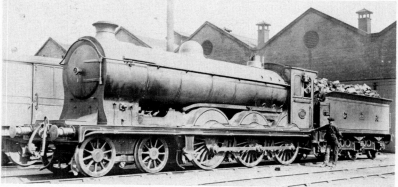

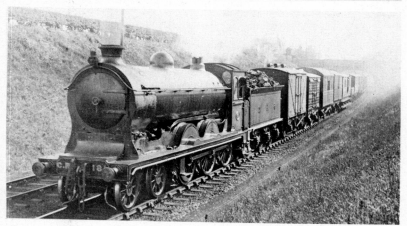

Top: McIntosh superheater 4-6-0 No 180 leaves Carlisle with a fast goods.
/F. E. Mackay

Centre: No 188 at Carlisle./*Rixon Bucknall Collection*

Bottom: No 181 of Balornock shed trundles past the camera on a mixed freight.
/Rixon Bucknall Collection

Top: McIntosh 'Oban Bogie' at Stirling in 1927./*P. Ransome-Wallis*

Above: An 'Oban Bogie' rebuilt with '918' boiler, LMS No 14606 at Oban shortly before withdrawal./*P. Ransome-Wallis*

Below: A '918' in LMS black livery./*P. Ransome-Wallis*

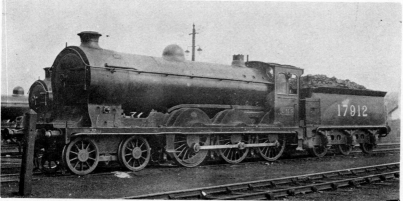

Top: A '908' in LMS red at Dalry Road, Edinburgh in 1928. The smokebox wingplates have been removed and the cab slightly modified by Pickersgill. */P. Ransome-Wallis*

Above: Even when black the '179s' looked elegant, as evidenced by No 17912. */Ian Allan Library*

Below: No 17913 in its final condition./*LPC*

Top: Belgian 'Oban Bogie' Type 35 4-6-0 No 3217 built by the Société de Haine in St Pierre, 1904. Basic design with 5ft 3in wheels and no superheater./*SNCB*

Above: The pioneer McIntosh *Dunalastair IV* 4-4-0 No 140.
/*Rixon Bucknall Collection*

Pickersgill '60' 4-6-0s

Top right: CR Pickersgill 4-6-0 No 63 speeds through Rockcliffe on the up Glasgow Diner./*H. Gordon Tidey*

Centre right: No 63 in repose at Carlisle, note the large balance weights.
/*Rixon Bucknall Collection*

Bottom right: Post-grouping '60' 4-6-0 built at St Rollox in 1926, in red livery. The tender is equipped with water pick-up./*Real Photographs Ltd*

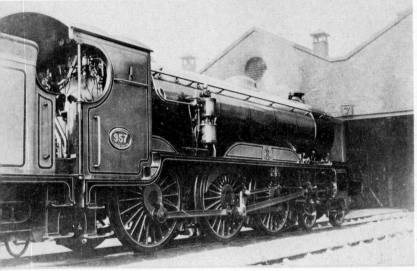

Top left: LMS-built '60' No 14647 in plain black livery. /*Ian Allan Library*

Centre left: Pickersgill '60' 4-6-0 No 54639 departs from Dundee with a freight on a golden autumn day in September 1948./*Gavin L. Wilson*

Bottom left: The month before its withdrawal the pioneer Pickersgill 4-6-0, and penultimate survivor, as BR No 54650 wheezes and clanks into Carlisle in August 1953./*J. Robertson*

Pickersgill '956' and '191' 4–6–0s

Top: Official portrait of Pickersgill CR three-cylinder 4-6-0 No 956./*LPC*

Above: An attractive study of No 957 on Carlisle Kingmoor Shed in 1922. /*A. B. Macleod*

Top: No 959 in full cry on the 12.30pm Aberdeen-Plymouth train./*Henry L. Salmon*

Above: An unidentified Pickersgill three-cylinder 4-6-0, almost certainly No 957 or 958, at Beattock Summit./*Rixon Bucknall Collection*

Top right: CR No 958 as LMS No 14802 in Derby red livery poses for the camera. Note the massive balance weights./*Ian Allan Library*

Centre right: Shortest lived of all the Pickersgill 4-6-0s was No 959, seen here as LMS No 14803. Visible is the vertical rocker shaft, a legacy of the derived valve gear originally fitted, retained merely as a valve spindle support./*LPC*

Bottom right: Maker's official photograph of Pickersgill 'Oban Bogie' 4-6-0 No 191. The firebox, although small, protruded substantially into the cab./*LPC*

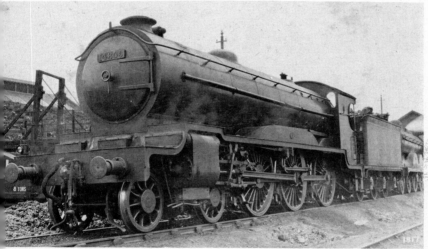

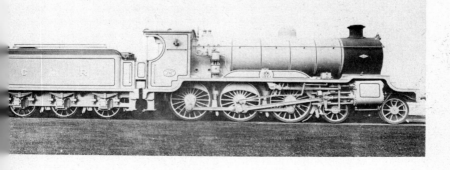

Top left: In original Caley blue livery Pickersgill 'Oban' 4-6-0 No 192 hurries along the main line near Stirling with a light train./*Rixon Bucknall Collection*

Centre left: A Pickersgill 'Oban' 4-6-0 in early LMS livery. Note the large balance weights, as with the preceding Pickersgill 4-6-0 designs these engines inflicted savage hammerblow on the permanent way./*P. Ransome-Wallis*

Bottom left: Two Pickersgill 'Oban Bogies' double-head an Edinburgh-Oban train in the Pass of Brander./*Ian Allan Library*

Manson G & SWR 4-6-0s

Top: A fine study of Manson G & SWR 4-6-0 No 386 stationed at Carlisle. /*Ian Allan Library*

Above: Immaculate No 386 at Carlisle Citadel Station./*Rixon Bucknall Collection*

Top left: Another Carlisle engine, No 381, seen fitted with a non-standard chimney having a capuchon./*Ian Allan Library*

Centre left: Official photograph of one of the rarely photographed Kilmarnock-built Manson 4-6-0s. Note altered brake rigging and cab and six-wheeled tender. /*W. D. Stewart Collection*

Bottom left: The same engine renumbered as 510 and reboilered by Whitelegg in 1920. Note also the new cab and bogie tender./*LPC*

Top: No 510 with its original tender pulls out of Carlisle with one of the so-called Midland 'Pullman' trains./*Rixon Bucknall Collection*

Above: Sister engine No 511 with capuchon chimney. The rodding to operate the variable blastpipe is clearly visible./*LPC*

Top left: No 509 newly rebuilt with extended smokebox by Whitelegg, but retaining its original boiler./*W. D. Stewart Collection*

Left: A vivid study of a Manson saturated steam 4-6-0 departing from Prestwick. /*M. W. Earley*

Top: Maker's portrait of one of the two Manson superheated G & SWR 4-6-0s of 1911./*Real Photographs*

Above: The second superheater 4-6-0, No 129, was built new fitted with the Weir feedwater heater and pump. The apparatus is clearly illustrated in this photograph. /*LPC*

Top: Manson No 129 with Weir apparatus removed and as renumbered 512 and modified by Whitelegg./*LPC*

Above: The same engine near the end of its days as LMS No 14674. Note the short outside steampipes, a very advanced feature when the engine was built. (1911). /*LPC*

drawbar pull must have been in the region of 5 tons, thereby amounting to 60-odd per cent of the nominal tractive effort.

Assuming grate area to be the cardinal dimension which determines a locomotive's maximum effort *pro rata*, a 6ft 6in 4-6-0 should have been able to haul the same load up the final 1 in 100 (always given in more recent years as 1 in 99) at a speed of 41mph, but there is no record of such a performance.

Of the '903' class the ill-fated No 907 would seem to have been a fine performer when new. The late R. E. Charlewood timed this engine on 378 tons tare/405 tons full from Strawfank Junction. The morning was fine and frosty and Summit was reached in 33min 26sec. The load was almost identical to that of 4-4-0 No 140 on that celebrated occasion two years earlier, and was conveyed between Elvanfoot and Summit in 4min 46sec, an average speed of 33.6mph. By Summit speed had fallen to only 31mph, rather than 41mph, which pointed to a cylinder output during the final stages of the ascent of around 1300-1350 hp.

A substantially greater effort of 1640 ihp was achieved by the same engine at the same location on a later run recorded by Rous-Marten in the *Railway Magazine* for September 1907. Here we read that 'A minimum rate of 50 miles an hour was sustained the greater part of the way to the Beattock Summit, and even up the last length, rising 1 in 100, the speed did not drop below 40 miles an hour, excepting fractionally and momentarily at the summit, I suspect through the driver notching up a little prematurely.'

This probably ranks as the greatest power output to be developed by a Caledonian locomotive working over its own metals. The geographical qualification has to be made, for on June 15, 1909, newly repaired after the Crawford derailment (see Chapter 11), No 903 *Cardean* materialised at Crewe, that Citadel of black locomotives, for a 25day sojourn on the LNWR. At the same time GNR large-boilered 4-4-2 No 1449 was experimentally working on the West Coast main line, mainly south of Crewe; unfortunately no photograph appears to exist of the two strangers together on Crewe North shed. Unfortunately, too, few details survive of No 903's exploits north of Crewe, but in the *Railway Magazine* for November 1936 O. S. Nock was able to publish some bare figures gleaned through the good offices of William Stanier.

On July 6, four days before the trials ended, *Cardean* headed the 9.15am train to Carlisle, arriving there 2min. late, which left only 23min to turn the engine before it returned south on the 12.58pm to Crewe. The train weighed 367 tons tare/390 tons full and made its first stop at Penrith ½min ahead of schedule. However, the 13.6 miles to Shap Summit were covered in 18½min, ½min *outside* the schedule. Nevertheless this was a tremendous effort involving an average output of 1465 ihp/1005 dbhp at 44mph.

In his book *The Caledonian Railway* and in the *Railway Magazine* for January 1963, O. S. Nock attempted to reconstruct a log showing the likely pass-to-pass times attained en route. This propounded an average speed of 49mph up the 7 miles of 1 in 125, which would have corresponded to an output of 1990 ihp/1380 dbhp! Taken at face value this represents an even greater level of output in relation to grate area than that attained by 4-4-0 No 140, and sustained for a longer duration. Of the two designs the smaller four-coupled engine actually had more ideal boiler proportions suited to an all-out sustained effort, whilst both engines would appear to have exceeded the ceiling of about 70 ihp/sq ft of grate attained by several modern superheated simple expansion locomotives throughout the world. At the overall average speed of 44mph, however, the effort up the 1 in 125 works out at a more realistic 1725ihp/1200 dbhp.

The work of No 903 on this occasion must have been quite out of character, but surely not such a great performance as Mr Nock suggests. On p.167-8 of his book he talks of edbhps of 1400-1500 sustained for 16min, which if considered in relation to the mean effort required are obviously rather too high for too long. Furthermore, no British 4-6-0 of this sort of capability was built until 1926-7, and sustained power outputs of this magnitude were not developed even by the LMS and BR Standard Class 5 4-6-0s of similar weight, which had larger and better proportioned superheated boilers *and* modern cylinder and valve gear design. The larger LNWR 'Claughton' superheated four-cylinder 4-6-0 No 1159 *Ralph Brocklebank,* which weighed 77¾ tons and had 30½sq ft of grate, on test north of Crewe in November 1913 developed only transitory actual maxima of 1669ihp and 1498dbhp (not at the same instant).

With quite unjustifiable precision, in view of the paucity of hard facts, and the uncertainty of resistance formulae, Nock goes on to remark that throughout the course of the run between Penrith and Shap Summit No 903 must have been developing a drawbar pull amounting to 61.2 per cent of its nominal tractive effort, thereby exceeding a corresponding figure of 60 per cent which he had once briefly experienced behind a GNR large-boilered 4-4-2 climbing Ardsley bank out of Leeds. It should be remembered that the Doncaster engine had a rather low tractive effort in relation to its ample boiler capacity, factors which did not unduly favour the St Rollox 4-6-0. The author's own calculations suggest that the drawbar pull would have risen to a maximum of about 4.7 tons ascending the 1 in 125 and so would not have exceeded 50 per cent of the nominal tractive effort. The fact remains that, quantitatively speaking, this must rank as probably the most outstanding effort to be made by a British steam locomotive in the pre-superheater era, which was all the more remarkable in view of the engine's only brief 'breather' at Carlisle following the 140-odd mile run up from Crewe earlier in the day.

Cecil J. Allen had an unrivalled experience of Caledonian express 4-6-0 performance both before and after superheating. In the *Railway Magazine* for June 1914 he remarked that on the basis of several runs 'no difference is apparent, unless it be in the slightest degree in favour of the engines as originally built.' Allen timed quite a number of runs behind the legendary No 903 itself, but one he would have 'given something for' was when he observed the engine on Easter Monday 1914 starting away from Carlisle unassisted at the head of 455 tons and noted that the speed of the last coach was at least 20mph when it passed the end of the platform. None of Allen's runs, however, would appear to have produced any efforts comparable with the early exploits of No 903 and 907 already related.

It is interesting that superheating apparently made such little difference to the performance of the big 4-6-0s, but it should be recalled that only three years elapsed between its provision and the outbreak of World War I. Also, during this brief period schedules had been slightly eased compared to the heady days of the Edwardian era. A former North Eastern engineman living near the author has observed that a superheater could be a mixed blessing to locomotives of this period (he had the Worsdell 'R' 4-4-0s particularly in mind) and could sometimes interfere with the steaming capabilities of a good saturated boiler whatever its other alleged benefits.

So far we have been preoccupied with the Glasgow-Carlisle main line. Few details survive of the exploits of the two Perth-based McIntosh 6ft 6in 4-6-0s, but in the *Railway Magazine* for September 1907 Rous-Marten briefly referred to No 904 taking a moderate 270 tons over the renowned fast 32½ mile stretch from Perth to Forfar in 36min 29sec at an average speed of 53½mph. Maximum speed was 67mph, which was somewhat pedestrain when compared to the famous 'even' timings achieved by 4-4-0s on the 'Tourist Express' over this section in the 1890s and subsequently.

At Perth No 904 had taken over its load, increased by 20 tons, from 5ft 9in 4-6-0 No 908 on the 'Grampian Express'. The smaller engine was reported to have run very freely at speeds of up to 65.2mph over the easier sections, and to have maintained a minimum speed of 31mph up Dunblane bank, where the maximum gradient is 1 in 78 for nearly ½mile commencing in a tunnel. This represented an effort of 1100 ihp/725 dbhp, which closely approximated to that by No 913 on 285 tons full timed by the late R. E. Charlewood in 1913. Here minimum speed on the slightly heavier load was 28mph, giving 1070 ihp/740 dbhp. A maximum speed of 65mph was noted down the 1 in 100 grade through Auchterarder. The work of these 5ft 9in 4-6-0s would thus appear to have fallen short of that of their 6ft 6in brethren, both 4-6-0 and 4-4-0. Their apparent maximum speed of 65mph was also somewhat on the low side when one considers that the 5ft 'Oban' 4-6-0s were early reported to be readily capable of 60mph down the banks, and that a 6ft 6in 4-6-0 could achieve 80mph.

Speed was certainly not a notable attribute of Pickersgill's 4-6-0s, which also developed dbhps that can rarely have broken into four figures. A run behind two-cylinder 4-6-0 No 61 on the 3.50pm ex-Glasgow express for Manchester and Liverpool was described by E. C. Poultney in *The Engineer* for October 15, 1920. The train, from Glasgow weighing 269tons tare, made a rather pedestrian run to Carstairs, where an eight-wheeler was removed and the Edinburgh portion was cut in, increasing the load to 389tons. The departure from Carstairs in a rain and hail storm was 16¾min late owing to the late arrival of the Edinburgh portion. Maximum speed during the ascent to Beattock Summit was 43.5mph at Abington, the final 1 in 100 being taken at an average speed of 32mph, latterly at 50per cent cut-off and half regulator.

The corresponding 10mile descent was made in a leisurely 11min 20sec with the regulator shut, at an average speed of only 53.5mph despite the lateness of the train. After a stop at Beattock the 17miles to Lockerbie were covered at an average speed of 50mph. At Lockerbie an eight-wheeler was removed, reducing the load to 365tons, which was then conveyed to Carlisle, 29.8miles, in 30½min, with a maximum of 60mph down the 1 in 200 near Gretna. Carlisle was reached 16½min late. The engine had therefore regained only ¼min of the 16¾min lost at Carstairs, allowing for which total running time was also ¼min inside the 170min then allowed between Glasgow and Carlisle. On the return run No 61, with 260tons tare, tackled Beattock bank unassisted at an average speed of 23.8mph and subsequently arrived in Glasgow 1min 5sec early.

Cecil J. Allen related a remarkably similar run behind the same engine on the same train in the *Railway Magazine* for January 1921. Again owing to the late arrival of the Edinburgh portion the departure from Carstairs was 21min late. With a load of 380tons Summit was passed at only 26mph and, following some very slow running down Beattock Bank, Carlisle was reached 20min late.

In both these runs, which must be regarded as typical, the engine showed a remarkable inability to regain lost time, fully confirming the sluggish reputation of the '60' class. History repeated itself in June 1926 when the first LMS-built '60', No 14630, ventured south of Carlisle to compete with the leading locomotive types of other LMSR constituents. Although the identity of the driver of No 903 in the 1909 trials is not known, that engine's subsequent driver, David Gibson, participated in the 1926 events. Despite the advantages of superheater and piston valves No 14630's performance fell well short of that of *Cardean* in that it took 20 min. to lift 350 tons from Penrith to Shap Summit, represented an average effort of 1190 ihp/810 dbhp. Shap bank was ascended at a minimum speed of 34mph and the drawbar pull did not exceed 4tons. During the course of the trials a maximum speed of 73mph was recorded descending towards Carlisle.

Of the locomotive types tested, the St Rollox 4-6-0 displayed the healthiest appetite for coal, both on a lb dbhp-hr basis, and in terms of lb/mile. The latter, at 51.6, was a surprisingly low figure nonetheless; although several months old the engine is reported to have covered only 7000-odd miles prior to the trials. The 66.3lb subsequently recorded as an average for the whole class in the rough and tumble of everyday service during 1928-1930, by which time these engines were largely employed on fast freight, would be far more representative of these 'miners' friends.'

LMSR locomotive trials: Preston-Carlisle 1926

	CR 60 4-6-0	MR Compound 4-4-0	LNWR 'Prince of Wales'	LYR 4-cylinder 4-6-0
Coal lb/DBHP hr*	5.19	4.25	5.05	5.07
lb coal/mile*	51.6	43.4	42.4	51.3
lb coal/mile 1928/1930	66.3	46.5	51.1	(59.7)†

* 350 ton trains

† E. S. Cox, *Chronicles of Steam* (Ian Allan 1967. p.115)

We now come to those fascinating failures, the Pickersgill three-cylinder 4-6-0s. In the *Railway Magazine* for August 1922 Cecil J. Allen related a run behind No 957 hauling a modest 260 tons full from Carlisle to Glasgow, which was reached dead on times despite two very severe signal checks and a conditional stop at Motherwell. Maximum speed recorded en route was 64½mph at Lockerbie, but at no stage from Carlisle to Summit were the pass-to-pass times better by more than 20sec., and at Beattock they were 35sec. behind those of Pickersgill 4-4-0 No 86 on 330 tons full tabulated alongside. Allen's verdict was that No 957's effort was 'a little disappointing.' He remarked that the engine's performance had not been exceptional and that 'it was clear from the comparatively muffled sound of the exhaust that No 957 was not being worked at anywhere near her full capacity.'

Nearly eighteen months later in the same journal for January 1924 we again find Allen behind No 957, which this time was hauling 315 tons full in the opposite direction. The same maximum speed of 64½mph was noted in the 'dip' at Lamington and a minimum of 43mph was measured over the 2 miles of 1 in 150 at Leggatfoot approaching Elvanfoot (1250 ihp/810 dbhp). The last 2.9miles to Summit were covered in 4min 35sec (average 38mph), by which point speed had dropped to 30½mph. The remaining 49.7miles to Carlisle were covered in 62min 5sec and Citadel was reached 1min 20sec ahead of schedule.

In the same article Allen tabulated a run with Pickersgill 4-4-0 No 96 on 405 tons full. It covered the 2.9miles from Elvanfoot to Summit (actual *mean* gradient 1 in 128) at an average speed of 37.2mph. This must have called forth an effort of at least 995 dbhp, which handsomely exceeds the maximum of 837 dbhp actually measured behind 4-6-0 No 14630 during the 1926 trials south of the Border.

The prototype three-cylinder 4-6-0, No 956, normally plied between Glasgow and Perth, but during May 1922 made some experimental runs to Aberdeen, and during the following autumn some trips between Glasgow Central and Carlisle. Driver Grassie took part in these trials, by which time the original derived valve gear had been replaced by Stephenson link motion, and on one such occasion in September 1922 he was joined on the footplate by the late Lord Monkswell and the Caledonian Locomotive Running Superintendent, John Barr. Notwithstanding the attendance of this distinguished assembly and Grassie's prowess, the engine steamed abominably and the round trip was abysmal. O. S. Nock delighted the reader with previously unpublished highlights from Monkswell's record in the *Railway Magazine* for January 1965. We are told that with 415tons full 'a remarkably poor ascent' was made of the bank ending at Craigenhill, and that the next 15miles were covered at an average speed of only 27mph, with boiler pressure hovering around the 160lb mark. Pressure plummeted to 125lb when the regulator was opened from half to full, a pressure which again obtained during the final stages of the climb to Summit. Here, incredibly enough, despite the lethargic performance, the train was virtually on schedule but still contrived to lose 2½min during the descent to Carlisle.

On the return journey with about 350 tons behind the tender No 956 reached Beattock 4min 10sec outside the 45min allowed and with assistance in the rear proceeded to labour up the 10miles to Summit in 31min 18sec, surely an all time Caledonian record! We are informed that latterly the engine was working 'all out' with full regulator and full forward gear with the pressure dropping to

130lb. Glasgow was eventually reached 15min late with no mitigating circumstances whatever, eg signal checks, to share the blame. In the twilight of the Caledonian's independent existence such a run was hardly a fitting climax on the line which had produced the 'Dunalastairs.'

Despite the bigger boiler and greater sophistication, in everyday service the '956' class proved to be no advance in haulage capacity over the earlier two-cylinder '60' class — if anything the reverse, as the result of the dual affliction of poor steaming and mechanical problems. The unassisted ascents of Beattock bank by No 61 described by Poultney, and by No 957 related by Cecil J. Allen, with both engines only loaded up to about 260tons behind the tender, simply bore no comparison with that achieved by No 50 with 330tons when brand new mentioned by Rous-Marten. The latter engine must have been developing an average of 950 dbhp for 19min, very good work indeed for 1903, whilst the improved 6ft 6in 4-6-0s of 1906, also using saturated steam distributed by slide valves, proved to be capable of a sustained 1000 dbhp. Although much of the former verve had gone out of Caledonian locomotive running, though the engines by then had the benefit of superheater and piston valves, this level of performance was unknown behind Pickersgill's 6ft 1in 4-6-0s. In terms of useful work done at the tender drawbar the latter did not normally aspire to some of the best efforts even of the 4-4-0s. However, on a special test run in 1922 No 956 is reputed to have hauled 420 tons gross from Carlisle to Beattock in 45¾min, an average speed of 52mph. This must have entailed a minimum sustained speed of at least 45mph up the 1 in 200 Gretna bank, which would have required an output in the region of 1000 dbhp, unusually good work for a Pickersgill 4-6-0.

Very little has been written of the actual performance of the Pickersgill 'New Oban Bogies', as they were officially designated. For a very detailed account of their exploits in July 1938 the author is indebted to R. Dyson of Urmston, Lancs, of which space permits only a brief abstract. By this period, ousted from the most important duties by the ex-HR 'Clans', half of the '191s' were shedded at Balornock and through locomotive working between Buchanan Street and Oban was in being. No 14620 (ex-CR 192) took 187tons tare/210tons full from Buchanan Street to Glenboig, 9 miles, in 14min 50sec as against a scheduled time of 16min. Following an intervening service slack Castlecary box was passed at 60mph, the maximum speed for the entire run, and the train was 2min ahead of time at Larbert, 22.1miles, where signals brought the speed down to 15mph. As a result Stirling, 30.2miles, was reached almost exactly on time.

A rather fitful run to Oban was then experienced with occasional bursts of speed scarcely exceeding 50mph, punctuated by numerous service slacks over the sharp curves. Over most sections beyond Killin Junction the train was about 2min ahead of schedule, and total running time over the 125 miles, Glasgow to Oban, was 52sec. inside the booked 222min. Mr Dyson's first-hand assessment of the '191' class at this time was that they seemed quite popular and that although 'in general the loads were not such as to tax this particular class unduly, they appeared to be quite ready to produce the extra power if there were any increase in loads to a reasonable degree.'

70

Caledonian Locomotive Performance
Elvanfoot—Beattock Summit (120ft rise in 2.9 miles)

Engine	Train weight tons	Speed	IHP	DBHP	Drawbar pull tons
4-4-0					
140 McIntosh	404F	36 S	1530	1145	5.3
96 Pickersgill	405F	37.2 A	1345 A	995 A	4.5 A
4-6-0					
49 McIntosh	390F	33 S	1400	995	5.1
907 McIntosh	405F	36.6 A	1380 A	975 A	4.5 A
		31 S	1350	965	5.2
907	350	40 S	1640	1120	4.7
61 Pickersgill	389T	32 A	1120 A	800 A	4.2 A
957 Pickersgill	315F	38 A	1215 A	800 A	3.5 A
		30.5 S	1115	735	4.0
ex-G&SWR Manson Superheater 4-6-0 (see Chapter 10).	365F	39 A	1420 A	1000 A	4.3 A

F — train weight full   T — train weight tare   A — average value, Elvanfoot-Beattock Summit
S — speed at Summit, effort calculated at this speed up 1 in 100 gradient.

Caledonian Locomotive Performance
Carlisle-Beattock-Beattock Summit

Engine	Train weight tons	Time, Carlisle-Beattock (39.7 miles) m.s.	Average speed mph	Time, Beattock-Summit (10.0 miles) m.s.	Average speed mph
4-4-0					
772 McIntosh *Dunalastair* II sup.	395F	47.15	50.4	21.25	28.0
86 Pickersgill sup.	330F	45.45	52.0	22.05	27.2
4-6-0					
McIntosh:					
49 sat.	390F	44.28	53.5	18.32	32.4
49 sat.	210F	43.45	54.5	20.15	29.6
50 sat.	330	(43.10)	(55.1)	19 *	31.6*
49 sup.	335F	45.06	52.8	20.10	29.9
903 sat.	305	44.30	53.5	18.45	32.2
903 sat.	335	45.15	52.7	20.15	29.6
903 sup.	335	49.40	48.0	19.45	30.4
903 sup.	390	47.10	50.5	20.35	29.2
906 ?	240	45.25	52.5	23.20	25.8
907 sat.	295	49.05	48.5	18.30	32.4
907 sup.	295	48.40	49.0	18.40	32.2
Pickersgill:					
61 sup.	260T	47.03	50.6	24.08*	23.8*
956 sup.	350	49.10	48.5	31.18	19.2
957 sup.	260F	46.20	51.4	21.40*	27.2*

* — unassisted Beattock-Summit   F — train weight full   T — train weight tare
sup. — superheated   sat. — saturated

To summarise, the work of the Caledonian 4-6-0s was rarely exceptional, sometimes good and frequently indifferent. For engines of their size and theoretical power, loadings were not unduly high nor schedules particularly demanding in relation to what was expected of the CR 4-4-0s. Indeed, the very fact that after nearly 20 years of development of the 4-6-0 type a moderately proportioned 4-4-0 could deputise and be preferred, was an indictment of the big six-coupled engines' shortcomings. To the casual observer, however, the latter were not immediately apparent concealed within an outer fabric of ethereal blue magnificence.

CHAPTER TEN

The Manson 4-6-0s of the G&SW

Whilst the Caledonian were building Nos 49 and 50 at St Rollox, elsewhere in Springburn, only half-a-mile away at the Atlas Works of Sharp Stewart & Co, no fewer than ten 4-6-0s were well under way for its bitter rival, the Glasgow & South Western. They were designed by the G&SWR Locomotive Superintendent, James Manson. By the time all were delivered during May 1903, 13 months after the order had been placed, the makers had joined forces a few weeks earlier with their two erstwhile rivals in Glasgow to form the huge North British Locomotive Company. The G&SWR 4-6-0s were thus amongst the very first locomotives to be turned out bearing NBL plates.

Although designed, built, and operated all but entirely in Scotland the new engines presented a remarkably un-Scottish appearance. They would have looked quite at home, say, on the Great Central, whilst over the next few years large numbers of 4-6-0s of very similar appearance were built for service on various railways in India. Unlike the two Caledonian machines, besides introducing the Belpaire firebox to Scottish railways as a whole, the new 4-6-0s made a complete break with previous G&SWR tradition by the adoption of outside cylinders. In this respect they smacked strongly of contemporary American practice, with Richardson balanced slide valves located in steam chests above the cylinders and outside the frames and actuated through rocker shafts from within by internal Stephenson valve gear. Steam reverse, a legacy from James Stirling's time, was provided in the cab. In a show of solidarity with its English partner, whose Pullman trains it took north from Carlisle, the Glasgow & South Western provided its 4-6-0s with large double-bogie tenders very similar to those attached by the Midland Railway to its largest 4-2-2s and 4-4-0s.

The Midland and Glasgow & South Western Railways endowed their locomotives with rather delicate proportions and did not believe in working them hard, preferring to treat them relatively gently uphill and gain time by fast descents. The more virile North Western/Caledonian axis experienced no such qualms and thrashed their engines mercilessly uphill, generating spectacle and sensational sound. Comparisons between the Caledonian and Glasgow & South Western 4-6-0 designs were and still are inevitable. Predictably perhaps, compared to the former the latter had a 'rather lean and hungry look', but in fact weighed only 3 tons less and was built to a comparable axleload limit of 18-18½ tons. It was also a better proportioned engine, and mechanically a superior proposition on account of the outside cylinders.

G&SWR locomotives in general tended to be overshadowed by those of the

Caledonian, not least the 4-6-0s. In more recent times these have generally bee،
dismissed as failures, or at best indifferent machines, largely on the strength of
accounts of pedestrian performance made when they were 15 or so years old
and well past their prime. In fact, in the context of their day the Manson 4-6-0s
were speedy and economical machines. They were limited to 245 tons unassisted
north of Kilmarnock and 335 tons south of there, yet trains of up to 430 tons
were by no means unknown, so the problem of double heading was not
eliminated by their arrival. Pilots were often as not slender domeless Hugh
Smellie 4-4-0s, which must have looked outmoded even in the early 1900s, but
which were nevertheless still regarded as good for reboiling years later—and in
some cases survived the 4-6-0s!

In 1905 Rous-Marten experienced some difficulty encountering a Manson
4-6-0 unpiloted yet well loaded up to its limit. However, he succeeded in timing
No 389 southbound at the head of 360tons to cover the 37 miles from New
Cumnock to Dumfries in 36min 27sec and to attain a maximum speed of
77½mph en route. On the return to Glasgow behind sister engine No 384, the
latter took 'approximately 400 tons' unaided from Carlisle to Dumfries, a distance of 33·1miles in 38min 4secs. This corresponded to an average speed of
52mph, whilst the maximum attained was 67¼mph on the fast approach to
Dumfries, where a pilot was attached.

The initial batch of ten engines was numbered 381 to 390. Of these Nos 381,
384-5, and 387-9 were allocated to Corkerhill shed in Glasgow. The remaining
three were at Currock Road shed, Carlisle. Seven more engines were built at
Kilmarnock during 1910-1911, numbered 119-120, 123-4, and 125-7. The first
four were sent to Corkerhill and had standard bogie tenders, whereas the final
three, which were allocated to Carlisle, were given six-wheeled tenders with no
diminution of coal or water capacity. The Kilmarnock-built engines differed
slightly from the NBL series; the brake rigging was completely redesigned, the
frames were deepened immediately behind the cylinders and the shape of the cab
was altered.

By the time the second series appeared economy measures were in force
which adversely affected maintenance and the 4-6-0s suffered as a consequence.
The outside cylinders had a tendency to work loose, and the smokeboxes drew
air, resulting in leaking tubes. This would suggest the front end was not as robust
as it might have been. A curious feature of all the G&SWR 4-6-0s adopted to
provide lateral clearance for the bogie and yet avoid either 'joggling' the frames
or deflecting them out of parallel, was that the front portion of the main frames
ahead of the coupled wheelbase was cut separately and lapped to the inside of
the rear section. Another feature was that the suspension of the main driving
axle was compensated with that of the rear coupled axle. After the original
engines had been in service some time, the weight distribution was modified
whereby 1¼tons were transferred off the bogie and on to the coupled wheels.
This roughly halved the variation in individual coupled axle loadings to nearly
1½tons, and actually reduced the maximum axleload to just below 18 tons.

Contemporaneous with the superheating by the Caledonian of its seven 6ft
6in 4-6-0s, two additional 4-6-0s were delivered to the G&SWR by NBL in July

1911, fitted with 21-element Schmidt superheaters and numbered 128 and 129. The second engine was equipped with a Weir feedwater heater and feed pump which were referred to as 'the distillery'. These two engines were directly developed from the earlier saturated design, boiler pressure being dropped from 180 to 160lb, and cylinder diameter was correspondingly increased from 20 to 21in. The latter had a record British width over clothing of 9ft 0¾in and so the cylinders had to be raised and slightly inclined. Piston valves of 10in diameter were provided, but the valve gear remained unchanged except that the steam lap was increased from 1in to 1¼in. An advanced, but seemingly hitherto un-remarked feature of these two engines was the use of outside steam pipes for the first time in British practice.

Despite these great improvements made in the front end it is rather surprising that the highest speed recorded behind a superheated G&SWR 4-6-0, 85mph, was scarcely greater than the 83mph experienced behind an unidentified (piloted) saturated 4-6-0 in wartime. Nevertheless, in terms of sheer haulage capacity the superheaters beat the others hands down and were sparkling performers, No 129 in particular. Cecil J. Allen often seemed to find himself behind this engine when travelling on the G&SWR. On the strength of one run made when it was still new he estimated that No 129 could have covered the 115½ miles from St Enoch to Carlisle non-stop in 125min thus equalling the rival Caledonian booked best time for their route, which was 13¼ miles shorter. As the two superheated 4-6-0s had to work the same trains to the same schedules as the standard machines it followed that they frequently gained time.

Manson sought to evaluate the relative efficacy of superheating and feedwater heating by pitting Nos 128 and 129 against a representative saturated stablemate from Corkerhill, No 123. Each engine made three round trips between Glasgow and Carlisle hauling 242 tons at an average speed of 50mph under the charge of the same driver. Compared to a coal consumption of 54½lb per mile by saturated No 123, superheated No 128 achieved 44½lb, a saving of 18 per cent. Following a reduction in blastpipe diameter from the standard 5½in to 4⅞in in order to divert steam into the heater, No 129 worked on a very economical 40½lb to the mile. The Weir apparatus was removed in 1919, and non-superheated No 389 was similarly fitted during 1913-1918, although no photographic record of this appears to exist.

It has always been a source of some surprise that additional superheated 4-6-0s were not built for the G&SWR, or that the earlier machines were not so converted. Manson retired immediately after the trials in November 1911 and was succeeded by Peter Drummond who, generally speaking, left his predecessors' engines well alone. For passenger duties Drummond commenced by ordering from NBL five very large inside-cylinder 4-4-0s which, lacking superheaters, were voracious coal eaters. Six similar engines fitted with superheaters, home-built a little later at Kilmarnock, were a great improvement, but with 20ton axleload all were dogged by mechanical troubles and were not entrusted for long with the principal main line duties. About 1914 Drummond outlined a massive four-cylinder 4-6-0 which mechanically resembled his late brother's later LSWR 4-6-0s, with cylinders in line abreast beneath the smokebox having divided drive, but which was endowed with an unusually large boiler smacking of Dugald's earliest 4-6-0s. Doubtless similarly difficult to fire, at 33sq ft, its long shallow grate would have been the largest of any current British passenger locomotive save the GWR *Great Bear*; a Robinson superheater would have been fitted following Peter Drummond's latter-day conversion to the principle. One or two superficial details, such as the triple-safety valve mounting, later found their way onto the celebrated 4-6-4 tank engines of 1922. The war deferred this interesting project and shortly before it might have seriously come under review Drummond died whilst still in office in June 1918.

When Robert H. Whitelegg (late of the LT&SR) took over at Kilmarnock a few weeks later, Manson's 4-6-0s were still the South Western's premier passenger locomotives and so they were to remain until 1922. In addition to working the main Anglo-Scottish services (to which the name 'Pullman' was still erroneously attached), they had also always worked some of the heavier Ayr trains. Following the provision of a larger turntable at Girvan in July 1913 they regularly worked further down the coast, but as the 50ft table at Stranraer could not accommodate them, the appearance of a 4-6-0 there was of the utmost rarity.

One of Whitelegg's first acts was to renumber logically the entire G&SWR locomotive stock, and the 4-6-0s became Nos 495 to 513 in chronological order during 1919. By this time the locomotive fleet was very badly run down as a result of the war and numerous Manson and Stirling 4-4-0s and 0-6-0s were reboilered and otherwise rebuilt. In March 1920 the last two non-superheated 4-6-0s, now Nos 510 and 511, were rebuilt with new boilers similar to the originals but having slightly longer fireboxes. New cabs were provided, but most noticeable were the extended smokeboxes which were also quickly applied to all the other 4-6-0s. For photographic purposes No 510 acquired, and retained for some years, a bogie tender, whilst No 511 was distinguished by a capuchon chimney. None of these alterations made any noticeable improvement upon performance, which had by now become mediocre.

Associated with the extended smokeboxes was Whitelegg's characteristic deep parallel chimney liner, which conferred indifferent steaming capabilities upon any locomotive on which it was inflicted. The 4-6-0s were now in a really poor way and in order to get them to steam a variable blastpipe device known as 'the razor' was installed, controlled from the cab. What was really required was complete and utter renewal, and following trials with a brand new Whitelegg 4-6-4T between Kilmarnock and St Enoch on the Anglo-Scottish services a scheme was got out late in 1922 to rebuild all the 4-6-0s with 'Baltic' boilers and cylinders. The result would have been a most handsome machine, as the accompanying drawing shows — virtually a tender version of the 4-6-4Ts, although little of the original engines could have remained except the tenders as new frames would have been essential. Regrettably the proposed metamorphosis was not proceeded with by the new management, under which, for some unaccountable reason, No 510 became LMS 14672 and No 511, LMS 14671!

Standard Midland Compound 4-4-0s soon took over the duties of the non-superheated 4-6-0s. The G&SWR locomotive shed at Carlisle (Currock Road) was almost immediately closed and its stock, almost unbelievably, moved to Kingmoor. Two of the 4-6-0s there with six-wheeled tenders, by now Nos 14670 and 14671, were moved to Dumfries and Hurlford (Kilmarnock) respectively about 1927.

In an attempt to bury the traditional hatchet further the two superheated 4-6-0s, which were blessed with more robust construction and an altogether livelier disposition than the other Manson 4-6-0s, worked for a period over the former Caledonian main line with some distinction. In the *Railway Magazine* for January 1929 Cecil J. Allen related secondhand a correspondent's run behind No 14674 (ex-129) on the 1.50pm ex-Glasgow Central hauling 365 tons full. For purposes of comparison with the data presented in the last chapter for CR engines the engine ascended from Elvanfoot to Summit at an average speed of 39mph. This corresponded to an estimated effort of 1420ihp/1000 dbhp, or a drawbar pull of 4·3 tons.

In 1927, following fracture of a trailing side rod, this engine ran as a 4-4-2 for a few weeks; it apparently suffered no apparent disadvantage despite a reduction in the adhesive factor from 5·9 to 4·0. No 14674 was ultimately the last former G&SWR 4-6-0 to survive and when condemned in November 1934 it had covered a total of 615,285 miles. The last of the saturated steam 4-6-0s to remain in service was No 14659, ex-G&SWR 384/498, until March 1933. In just under thirty years it had aggregated 858,303 miles. James Manson lived to witness the demise of virtually all his locomotives, the 4-6-0s included, for he died in Ayrshire in June 1935 at the age of 90.

Although Manson would have held overall responsibility, it seems probable that the detailed design of his original 4-6-0s was worked out by the makers. The engines bore a strong superficial resemblance to twelve 5ft 6in gauge passenger 4-6-0s completed at Atlas in 1902 for the Bengal Nagpur Railway, but which had inside steamchests. Rather curiously, in describing the latter in its March 7, 1903 issue *The Locomotive* erroneously stated that 'the motion is Stephenson link, the valves being placed on top of the cylinders and worked by a rocking shaft' — a description that exactly fitted the 4-6-0s for the Glasgow & South Western Railway, then under construction.

G&SWR No	Date	Builder	G&SWR 1919 No	LMS No	Date scrapped
381	1903	NBL 15734	495	14656	
−390		−15743	−504	− 14665	1928-1933
119, 120	1910	Kilmarnock	505	14666	
123-125			−509	−14670	
126, 127	1911	Kilmarnock	510†, 511†	14672, 14671	
128	1911	NBL 19504	512	14673	1933
129	1911	NBL 19505	513	14674	1934

† rebuilt 1920

CHAPTER ELEVEN

A Chapter of Accidents

The Scottish 4-6-0 enjoyed a remarkably good public safety record, for only one was ever involved in an accident which resulted in the deaths of passengers. The engine concerned, CR No 907, although stationary at the time, had the misfortune to be damaged beyond repair in the terrible double collision at Quintinshill, near Gretna in May 1915, which had the grim distinction of being by far the worst disaster in British railway history.

Six years earlier, at about half-past nine in the evening of 2 April, 1909, sister engine No 903 *Cardean* also very nearly came to grief. At the head of the down 'Corridor' it had just passed Crawford station and was descending the 1 in 240 grade at a speed of at least 60mph when the engine suddenly parted company from the tender. Both enginemen were mercifully standing on the footplate, Fireman Alcorn's attention being concentrated on a malfunctioning injector. Driver Currie immediately attempted to apply the Westinghouse brake, which also came into operation automatically, and tried to put the engine into reverse gear, to no avail. However the engine came to rest about ¾ mile further on. Investigation showed that it had nine wheels still on the rails, but of the left-hand driving wheel there was no sign! The main frames were twisted and bent, the reversing gear wrenched away and the brake rigging disarranged. The errant wheel, with a portion of coupling rod attached, was eventually discovered leaning against a boundary fence, which it had partially demolished, close by the 56th mile post and about 150 yards beyond the point where the crank axle had evidently fractured.

What of the remainder of the train? The Westinghouse brake having immediately come into operation its speed was reduced from at least 60mph to zero in 250yds or about 17secs. Much of its kinetic energy was absorbed by the track ballast for the tender and all the coaches were derailed, being displaced to one side of the track or the other, but they remained in an upright position. The first four vehicles and the tender came to rest fouling the up line, whilst after a gap of 20yds the remaining five vehicles finished up on the other side of the track jammed up against the side of the 3ft-deep cutting. There was considerable damage to the permanent way over some distance with rails torn up. Ten passengers complained of shock.

The villain of the piece appeared to be the crank axle, which had been manufactured in Newcastle-upon-Tyne in February 1906 by John Spencer & Sons Ltd. It had been put into No 903 when new in May 1906 and had accrued 145,389 miles prior to failure. It was covered by a 200,000mile guarantee and had fractured at the point where the axle suddenly increased from 8½in to 9½in diameter as it entered the wheel boss. Microscopic metallurgical examination of the crank axle material promptly followed and indicated excessive quantities of carbon, manganese sulphide and manganese silicate, which had the effect of rendering the metal brittle. Ironically, although the railway specification required certain physical characteristics to be fulfilled, no specific chemical content was called for. The official report found that the steel had not been manufactured with sufficient care, but also recommended that sudden changes of axle diameter with associated sharp angles between journal and wheel seat should be avoided in the future. The report referred to the fact that two crank axles of 'similar design' had failed on the CR in February 1909 and April 1908, having respectively covered 66,379 and 147,574 miles. These axles had been produced by two other different manufacturers, but the identities of the engines concerned were not revealed.

In its issue for June 25, 1909 *The Engineer* validly criticised Colonel Yorke's report on account of the fact that it did not satisfactorily explain why the coupling had broken between the engine and tender. He had attributed this to the lurch the engine would have given the instant the crank axle failed. However, a lurch of sufficient magnitude to have achieved this would hardly have permitted the engine to remain on the rails as it did. *The Engineer* suggested a broken rail as possibly having precipitated the near disaster. The fracture would have remained undetected amidst the subsequently badly damaged track, and could have caused the coupling rod to break *before* the crank axle. Even so, the precise sequence of events during those alarming few seconds has never been satisfactorily explained in relation to the nature of the damage sustained by the engine.

It was a mercy that this alarming occurence resulted in no serious ill-effects to anyone and that it did not occur three months later when the engine was storming toward Shap on the LNWR at maximum output. If it had occured there the damage to Caledonian prestige alone would have been great. As it was, the CR could feel proud of the diligence of its servants. The driver had reacted immediately in trying to bring the engine to a stop, after which the fireman had hastened forward to Abington with lamp and detonators to warn any approaching train and to summon help. The two guards in the train had immediately sought to protect the disabled train fore and aft with detonators and to raise the alarm at Crawford. Special praise was due to the Signalman Brownrigg at Abington, who had wisely held an up goods when it arrived eight minutes after the 'Corridor' should have passed, and ten minutes after the express was known to have entered the section, 2½miles to the south, thereby averting a collision.

Such devotion to duty was not apparent near Gretna on May 22, 1915. At about six o'clock on that fateful morning 4-6-0 No 907 departed from Carlisle on a lightweight stopping train. The engine was running in after overhaul, otherwise its regular early morning duty would have been to take over the 11.45pm ex-Euston from the LNWR at Carlisle. On this particular morning the latter was running half an hour late and so the local was permitted to amble on ahead instead of behind it.

To give the overdue express a clear path, however, the local was shunted on to the up main line upon reaching Quintinshill signalbox just north of Gretna, both refuge loops already being occupied. This procedure was not unusual and Fireman Hutchinson stepped down from the footplate to sign the log book as prescribed by Rule 55. He was accompanied by Signalman Tinsley, who had unofficially been 'picked up' at Gretna and who should have relieved Signalman Meakin, with whom he had a 'special arrangement', half an hour earlier at six o'clock. The latter, upon admitting the local on to the up main line, had omitted to place a 'collar' upon the signal lever as a precaution against inadvertently pulling off the up home and distant signals. He had also failed to inform his colleague in Kirkpatrick box, nearly 3 miles to the north, of his action. Meakin's failure to observe these vital precautions was overlooked by Hutchinson, who left the box to return to his engine.

Oblivious of the blue 4-6-0 and train, upon which he had just travelled on the footplate and which was standing only yards away, Tinsley gave the 'all clear' to a troop train headed by 4-4-0 No 121, which was approaching at speed on the up line. The impact was horrific and reduced the troop train to almost one third of its original length. Only a minute later, when it was too late to avert further disaster, the overdue express from the south burst on the scene at about 60mph, double-headed by 4-4-0s Nos 140 and 48, which ploughed into and over the wreckage. Then came the crowning horror — fire. Cinders spilled from the battered locomotives' ashpans and ignited the wooden carriages, several of those of the troop train being illuminated by gas compressed in cylinders. A raging inferno ensued; even the coal in the locomotive tenders caught fire and burned for 24hr, whilst thousands of gallons of valuable water gushed to waste from the ruptured tender tanks.

No fewer than 227 people died in the holocaust, several incinerated beyond trace, of whom 214 were military personnel otherwise destined for the carnage at Gallipoli. The locomotives involved were towed back to St Rollox, where 4-4-0s Nos 140 and 48 were eventually repaired. Similar attempts were made without success to resurrect the other two engines, which had taken the full impact. The boiler of the big 4-6-0 had been ruptured, its cylinders smashed, its main frames damaged and its tender battered. The remains were cut up in January 1916 and no new Caledonian engine ever subsequently bore the number 907, although 4-4-0 No 121 was replaced by a new Pickersgill four-coupled engine bearing the same number.

The Crawford accident was directly attributable to a mechanical failure, and that at Quintinshill to a signalman's human error. The last accident to involve a Scottish 4-6-0 was a result of a combination of both factors, and oddly enough occured at a point almost exactly mid-way between Quintinshill and Crawford. The place was Dinwoodie, and the date October 25, 1928.

Following a day of domestic tribulation, Signalman Scott in Wamphray box accepted the Carlisle-Dundee express goods from his colleague in Dinwoodie box 2½ miles to the south. He immediately gave the 'train entering section' signal to Murthat box to the north in order to allow himself a few minutes' sleep.

The goods was hauled by Pickersgill '60' 4-6-0 No 14631 (one of the post-grouping built series) and about ¾ mile beyond Dinwoodie box the engine was obliged to stop. The small connecting rod, which took the drive off a return crank on the left hand trailing coupled wheel to operate the mechanical lubricator on the footplate, had come adrift. During the course of repairs the previous afternoon a fitter had omitted to fix a split pin to make the connection secure owing to the absence of a hole in the nut. The guard of the disabled goods train belatedly and leisurely made his way forward to ascertain the cause of the trouble. Having discovered this he set about protecting the rear of the train with detonators.

Meanwhile, dozing by his fire in the comfort of Wamphray box 1¾ miles to the north, Signalman Scott was roused from his slumbers by an enquiry from Dinwoodie box as to whether the line was clear for the 'Royal Highlander' express, which was approaching from the south. Scott assumed that the goods had passed him during his period of drowsy inattention and gave the 'all clear'. As a result the express, double-headed by Midland compound No 1176 and 4-4-0 No 14435 (ex-CR 900) ploughed into the rear of the stationary goods in the darkness.

The passenger train itself was scarcely damaged and its passengers uninjured, but the four enginemen were all killed. Among them by a curious quirk of fate was John Cowper, whose father as driver of 4-4-0 No 140 had been injured at Quintinshill and almost certainly later died as a direct consequence of that accident. Both 4-4-0s were very badly damaged and the former CR engine was immediately scrapped. The Pickersgill 4-6-0, however, which had not been directly involved, survived for almost another 20 years.

CHAPTER TWELVE

Some Notes on Names

The Highland Railway named its passenger locomotives extensively, the Caledonian only sparingly and the Glasgow & South Western not at all (with the exception of one 4-4-0 in 1922). Scottish practice generally was to paint names on locomotive splashers, rather than affix brass nameplates as was customary in England. This was a contributory factor to the short-lived nature of certain of the very few names carried by CR engines, probably all of which had already disappeared before 1923.

Sir James Thompson (CR No 50) originally joined the CR as a goods clerk in 1850 when a boy of fourteen. He rose to become Goods Manager in 1870 and General Manager in 1882, a post he held until 1900. He was knighted in 1897 and was Chairman of the Caledonian Railway from 1901 until his death in June 1906.

Cardean (CR No 903) was the Perthshire estate near Alyth Junction of Edward Cox who, at the time the engine was named, was merely a director on the Board, but who later became Deputy Chairman. Oddly enough in CR days *Cardean* itself would rarely if ever have been seen in the Perth area, although two identical sister engines were stationed there. A nameless working model of No 903 which was made by W. H. Cox, who was latterly Chairman of the Highland Railway, is exhibited in Perth Museum. In 1920 the name was reported to have been removed from No 903.

Sir James King (CR No 909) was appointed Chairman after the death of Sir James Thompson only a few days after *Cardean* would have been named, but rather oddly had to be content with one of the smaller 5ft 9in 4-6-0s. He retired in September 1908, and the name was removed from the engine sometime after his death in 1911.

Barochan (CR No 911) was the name of the home near Houston, Renfrew, of Sir Charles Bine Renshaw, Deputy Chairman. He succeeded Sir James King as Chairman, which he remained until his death in March 1918, after which the name was probably removed.

In contrast to the formidable Gaelic names of some of the Drummond 4-4-0s, the Highland passenger 4-6-0s had straightforward names which did not lend themselves to mis-spelling during the course of repaints at either St Rollox or Kilmarnock Works (as sometimes happened with the smaller engines, to the chagrin of Highlanders).

Taymouth Castle (HR No 140) near Aberfeldy was the seat of the Marquis of Breadalbane, who had a seat on both the Highland and Caledonian Boards (and who was probably the 'go-between' in the sale of the 'River' 4-6-0s).

Ballindalloch Castle (HR No 141) in Banffshire, was the seat of the Macpherson Grant family.

Dunrobin Castle (HR No 142) near Golspie, was the seat of the Duke of Sutherland, an HR director.

Gordon Castle (HR No 143), on the borders of Banff and Moray, was the seat of the Duke of Richmond and Gordon.

Blair Castle (HR No 144) near Blair Atholl, was the seat of the Duke of Atholl, an HR director.

Murthly Castle (HR No 145) is on the HR main line near Stanley north of Perth.

Skibo Castle (HR No 146) is on the Dornoch Firth near Dornoch, and was the home of Andrew Carnegie the philanthropist.

Beaufort Castle (HR No 147) is near Beauly on the River Beauly, and was the seat of Lord Lovat, an HR director.

Cawdor Castle (HR No 148) is near Nairn, and was the seat of the Earl of Cawdor.

Duncraig Castle (HR No 149) is on Loch Carron, near Strome Ferry.

Dunvegan Castle (HR No 30) is on Skye, and was the seat of Clan Macleod.

Urquhart Castle (HR No 35) is a ruined castle on the shores of Loch Ness.

Brahan Castle (HR No 26), near Dingwall, is associated with the legend of the Brahan seer.

Thurso Castle (HR No 27) was the seat of the Sinclairs of Ulbster.

Cluny Castle (HR No 28) on the River Spey near Kingussie, was the seat of the Cluny Macphesons.

Dalcross Castle (HR No 43/29) near Inverness, was an ancient baronial castle.

Brodie Castle (HR No 50) near Forres, was the seat of the Brodie family since the mid-11th century.

Darnaway Castle (HR No 58) near Forres, was the seat of the Earl of Moray.

Foulis Castle (HR No 59) near Dingwall, was the seat of Clan Munro (qv).

River Ness (HR No 70) is the 7mile long river carrying the outflow of Loch Ness into the Moray Firth at Inverness.

River Spey (HR No 71) is the fastest flowing and second longest river in Scotland (107 miles). It rises at Loch Spey and enters the Moray Firth between Lossiemouth and Buckie.

Clan Campbell (HR No 49) attained no little notoriety by the massacre, under the orders of King William III of England, of members of Clan Macdonald in February 1692, at Glencoe.

Clan Fraser (HR No 51) is of French origin dating back to c. 12th century.

Clan Munro (HR No 52) is an ancient clan, whose seat is Foulis Castle (above), and who fought on the Hanoverian side during the 1745 uprising.

Clan Stewart (HR No 53) is the Royal clan, of Norman French origin. The direct male line ended with the death of King James V of Scotland in 1542, but succeeding claimants to the Scottish throne profoundly influenced Scottish and English history during the 16th, 17th and 18th centuries, their hopes finally being smashed at the 40min Battle of Culloden in April 1746.

Clan Chattan (HR No 54) is a composite clan which encompasses several clans, including Mackintosh and Macpherson.

Clan Mackinnon (HR No 55) is a clan formerly with lands on the islands of Mull, Skye and Arran, who fought beside the Stuarts in 1745.

Clan Mackenzie (HR No 56) is an ancient clan, possibly of Irish origin.

Clan Cameron (HR No 57) is a clan who assisted in the Jacobite victory at the Battle of Killiecrankie in July 1689, and who subsequently fought strongly for the Stuart cause.

Of the eight 'Clan' names, five — those of *Campbell, Fraser, Stewart, Mackenzie* and *Cameron* — subsequently reappeared on 4-6-2 engines of BR Standard Class 6, of which ten were built at Crewe during 1951-2. The latter were originally designed with thoughts of service between Perth and Inverness, but this never came to pass and they generally worked south of Glasgow. Unlike its illustrious Highland forebear, the BR 'Clan' was somewhat shy of steam, but with the benefit of modern cylinder and valve gear design it was decidedly more fleet of foot and was altogether a much bigger engine. It also enjoyed a much shorter working life, for it disappeared during the holocaust of dieselisation, which also swept to the breaker's yard LMS and BR 4-6-0s, the worthy and more efficient, but less attractive successors of the Scottish 4-6-0.

Postscript

Since the manuscript for this book was completed, copies of numerous locomotive drawings and diagrams have become obtainable through the Oxford Publishing Company. A number of these relate to unfulfilled locomotive projects, particularly with respect to the former Caledonian Railway. Several have previously never been referred to in print.

A number of these projects are admittedly schemes alternative to those which actually went into production. For instance, it is evident that the McIntosh 'Oban' 4-6-0 was also schemed with 5ft 6in coupled wheels, thus forshadowing Pickersgill's indifferent successors to the engines as constructed with 5ft coupled wheels.

Before these first St Rollox 4-6-0s were built, McIntosh was already thinking in terms of a main line 4-4-2 passenger engine. A diagram dated September 1901 shows such an engine, which in general proportions is not very far removed from the two 6ft 6in 4-6-0s Nos 49 and 50 built 18 months later, except that its weight in working order was somewhat optimistically estimated at only 63½tons without tender. Similarly McIntosh's projected inside-cylinder 4-4-2 of May 1905 would have closely resembled the '903' 4-6-0s turned out the following year, but would have had a slightly deeper firebox and a boiler barrel more sensibly constructed in only three telescopic rings. In his recently published definitive work *Forty Years of Caledonian Locomotives 1882-1922* (David & Charles 1974) H. J. Campbell Cornwell states that five such 4-4-2s were authorised in November 1905 for service between Edinburgh and Carlisle, and between Carlisle, Perth and Aberdeen.

In this excellent book the author also states that the Pickersgill '60' class was directly derived from a projected McIntosh superheated 6ft 6in 4-6-0 of 1911, which was to have had 21in by 26in outside cylinders. A smaller 65ton, 5ft 9in express goods 4-6-0 was also outlined in similar mould with 20½in by 26in. cylinders and a superheated version of the original '55' class boiler. With the footplate neatly stepped over the inclined cylinders this badly underboilered proposal could similarly have been a basis for the Pickersgill 'New Oban Bogie', which was very similar in profile. (Alternatively, the addition of a trailing truck, side tanks and bunker virtually result in a 'Wemyss Bay' tank).

Another scheme intended for the same duties as the express goods 4-6-0 was a 56 ton 5ft 9in 2-6-0, which was to have had a superheated 4-4-0/0-6-0 pattern boiler with the firebox between the coupled axles. Dated February 1912, this proposal was to have had outside cylinders measuring either 19½in by 26in or 18¾in by 28in and could well have been quite a useful engine. In the event of course, a superheated version of the '908' class, the '179' class, was built, but for which it is tempting to suggest that in the wake of the Crawford accident McIntosh had had second thoughts about the employment of inside cylinders in future large six-coupled locomotives. His sudden interest in outside cylinders at his eleventh hour is otherwise puzzling, but at this distance in time we can only speculate.

In *The North British Railway Vol 2* (David & Charles 1975) John Thomas mentions that Cowlairs under W. P. Reid had designed a large 4-6-0 for the 'Waverley Route', which was shelved as an economy measure. This machine, more obliquely referred to in his earlier book on the NBR Atlantics, had been designed in the summer of 1907 for service between Edinburgh and Carlisle following severe criticism by the Civil Engineer, James Bell, of the rough riding qualities of Reid's 4-4-2s and their allegedly adverse effect upon the track. No doubt with enhanced stability in mind there was to be a reversion to inside cylinders, which would have contained coned pistons with tail rods, and had slide valves mounted on top worked through rocker shafts. The proposed NBR 4-6-0 would have strongly resembled the Caledonian '903' class; its boiler would have been directly developed from that of the 4-4-2s, with a fourth ring added to the front end of the barrel into which the smokebox tubeplate would have been recessed. The Belpaire firebox would have been slightly shorter, giving a nominal grate area of 27.7sq ft, which in the course of a long run could have been reduced to an effective 19sq ft or so. The ashpan beneath the rear third of the firebox would have been very restricted and without benefit of a back damper, unlike the corresponding Caledonian engines, the published drawings of which must have been examined at Cowlairs.

The big 6ft 6in North British 4-6-0 should have been rather heavier than the latter and compared to its brother 4-4-2s would have had the advantage of an extra probable 17-18 tons of adhesive weight. However, simply because of the reasons given above, in performance it is doubtful if the projected 4-6-0 would have shown up to any advantage over the Carlisle road, when compared to the Atlantics which had at last found favour by the time the NBR economy improved and more big engines were required.

To end upon a picturesque note, another 'explanation' of the louvred locomotive chimneys of David Jones has come to light in *The Locomotive* for March 21, 1903. Here we read that by lifting the exhaust his intention had been 'to save the beautiful views on his railway for the tourist passengers' enjoyment.' (As Jones does not appear to have patented the idea, there exists no specification from which to glean the definitive explanation). Characteristically, Peter Drummond showed no such touching concern for the delicate sensibilities of the clientele, but for the 'Rivers' F. G. Smith thoughtfully specified vacuum ejector exhaust silencers of a simple pattern which he had patented jointly with the Vacuum Brake Co. in 1913.

Appendix

Data from the Report of the Bridge Stress Committee, 1928. (The Report proposed that total locomotive hammerblow should not exceed 12½ tons at 5rps in future British locomotives).

Class	Driving Wheel dia	Max. Axle-load tons	Axle Hammerblow at 6rps tons	Max Combined Loading at 6rps tons	Total Locomotive Hammerblow at 6rps tons	Speed at 6rps mph
CR 908	5ft 9in	18.0	6.9	24.9	10.5	74
CR 179	5ft 9in	18.25	8.0	26.25	6.4	74
CR 191	5ft 6in	15.7	11.0	26.7	26.9	71
CR 60	6ft 1in	19.3	11.7	31.0	23.5	78
HR 75	5ft 3in	13.9	6.3	20.2	16.6	67
HR 'Castle'	5ft 9in	15.15	6.2	21.35	16.3	74
HR 'Castle'	6ft 0in	15.45	8.0	23.45	16.3	77
HR 'River'	6ft 0in	17.75†	4.2	21.95	1.7	77
HR 'Clan'	6ft 0in	15.33	7.1	22.43	15.3	77
LSWR H15	6ft 0in	19.85	10.5	30.35	25.5	77
GWR 'Saint'	6ft 8½in	18.4	6.9	25.3	17.9	86

* These values are largely theoretical, very few of the locomotives listed in the Report could have attained a rotational speed of 6rps on account of short travel valves and poor front end design.

† CR/LMS engine diagrams, the HR Engineers Dept. diagram dated September 1915 gave 17.33 tons.

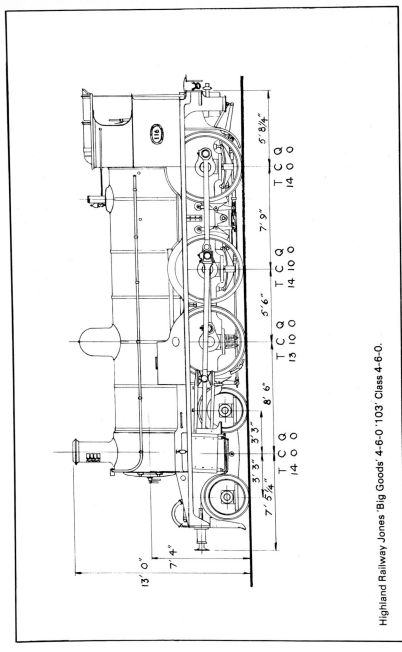

Highland Railway Jones 'Big Goods' 4-6-0 '103' Class 4-6-0.

Jones 4-6-0

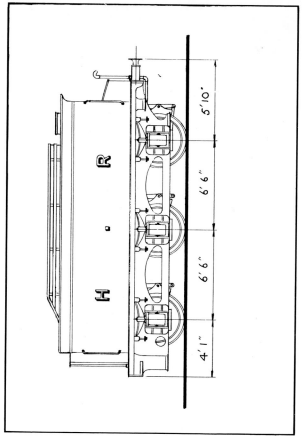

Railway	HR
Class	'103'
Cylinders (in)	20×26
Driving Wheel Dia	5ft 3in
Boiler Pressure (lb)	170
Max Boiler Dia	4ft 9in
Tube Length	14ft 1½in
Tube Heating (Sq ft.)	1,559
Firebox	114
Total Evaporative	1,673
Superheater	—
Grate Area	22.6
Adhesion Weight(tons)	42.0
Engine Weight	56.0
Tender Weight	38.35
Coal Capacity (tons)	5
Water Capacity (gals)	3000
Tractive Effort (lb)	24,500
Overall Length	58ft 4½in

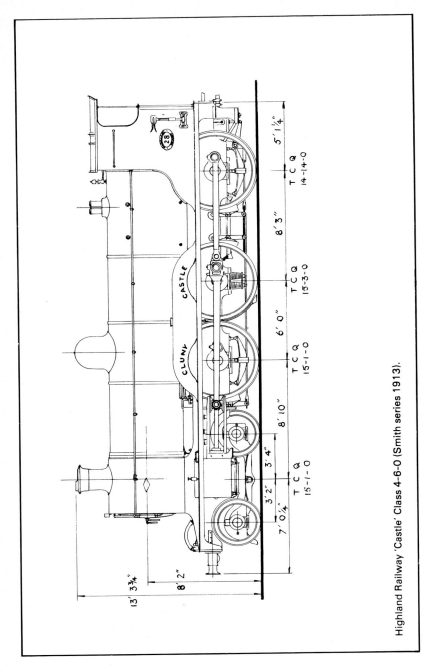

Highland Railway 'Castle' Class 4-6-0 (Smith series 1913).

Highland Rly 'Castle' 4-6-0

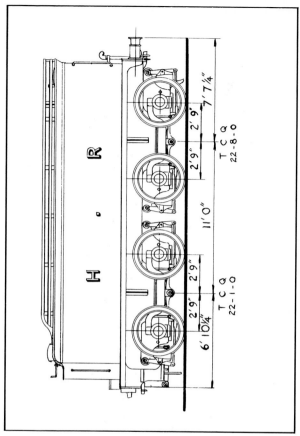

Railway/Class	HR 'Castle'		
Batch	1900	1913	1917
Cylinders (in)	19½×26	19½×26	19½×26
Driving Wheel Dia	5ft 9in	5ft 9in	6ft 0in
Boiler Press.(lb)	180	180	180
Max Boiler Dia	5ft 0in	5ft 0in	5ft 0in
Tube Length	14ft 9⅜in	14ft 9⅜in	14ft 9⅜in
Tube Heating			
Surface (sq ft)	1,916	1,916	1,916
Firebox	134	132	132
Total Evaporative	2,050	2,048	2,048
Superheater	—		
Grate Area	26.5	25.5	25.5
Adhesion Wt (tons)	43.85	44.9	46.35
Engine Wt (tons)	58.85	59.95	60.65
Tender Wt (tons)	44.45	44.45	46.35
Coal Cap. (tons)	5	5	6½
Water Cap. (Gal)	3,350	3,350	4,000
Tractive Effort (lb)	21,900	21,900	21,000
Overall length	60ft 7in	60ft 7in	60ft 9½in

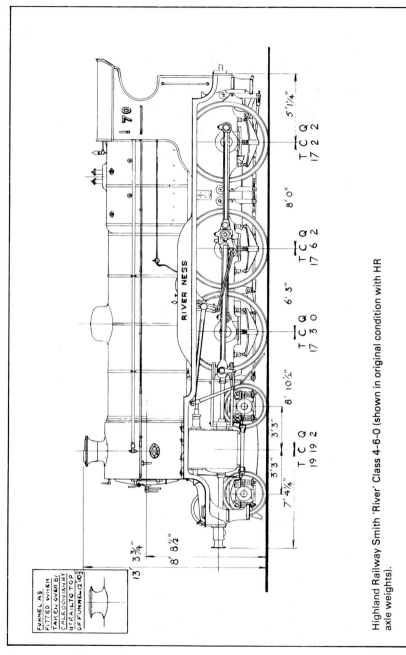

Highland Railway Smith 'River' Class 4-6-0 (shown in original condition with HR axle weights).

Smith 'River' 4-6-0

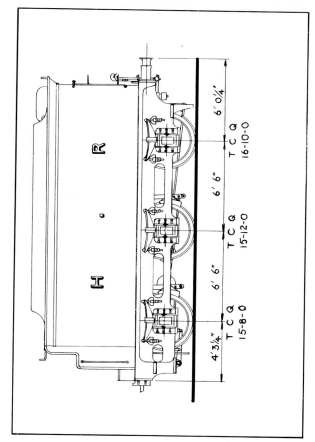

Railway	HR	CR	LMSR
Class	diagram	diagram	diagram
Cylinders (in)		21×28	
Driving Wheel Dia		6ft 0in	
Boiler Pressure (lb)		160	
Max Boiler Dia		5ft 3in	
Tube Length		14ft 9in	
Tube Heating			
Surface (sq. ft.)		1,460	
Firebox		140	
Total Evaporative		1,600	
Superheater		350	
Grate Area		25.3	
Max. Axleload (tons)	17.33	17.75	17.75
Adhesive Wt (tons)	51.6	53.0	52.5
Engine Weight (tons)	71.6	72.3	71.9
Tender Weight (tons)	47.5	49.2	47.5
Coal Capacity (tons)		6½	
Water Capacity (gals)		4,000	
Tractive Effort (lb)		23,300	
Overall length		59ft 6in	

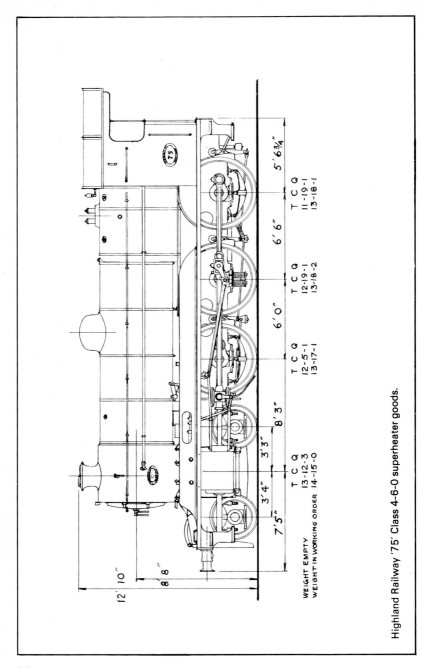

Highland Railway '75' Class 4-6-0 superheater goods.

Highland Railway 'Superheater Goods' 4–6–0

Railway	HR
Class	'75'
Cylinders (in)	20½×26
Driving Wheel Dia.	5ft 3in
Boiler Pressure (lb)	175*
Max Boiler Dia	4ft 7¾in
Tube Length	14ft 1¼in
Tube Heating Surface (sq ft)	1,069
Firebox	130
Total Evaporative	1,199
Superheater	241
Grate Area	22.75
Adhesion Weight (tons)	41.7
Engine Weight (tons)	56.45
Tender Weight (tons)	35.65
Coal Capacity (tons)	5
Water Capacity (gals)	3,000
Tractive Effort (lb)	25,800
Overall Length	55ft 5in

* Originally 160lb.

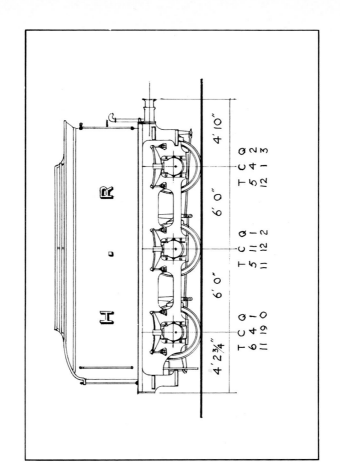

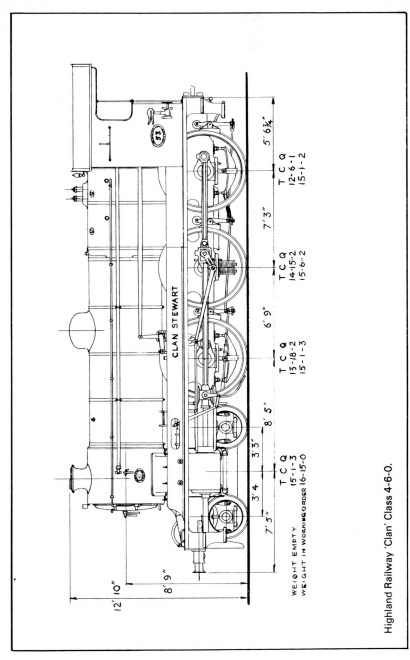

Highland Railway 'Clan' Class 4-6-0.

Highland Railway 'Clan' 4-6-0

Railway	HR
Class	'Clan'
Cylinders (in)	21 x 26
Driving Wheel Dia.	6ft 0in
Boiler Pressure (lb)	175lb
Max. Boiler Dia	4ft 9¾in
Tube Length	14ft 10⅛in
Tube Heating Surface (sq. ft.)	1,328
Firebox	139
Total Evaporative	1,467
Superheater	256
Grate Area	25.5
Adhesion Weight (tons)	45.5
Engine Weight (tons)	62.25
Tender Weight (tons)	42.05
Coal Capacity (tons)	7
Water Capacity (gals)	3,500
Tractive Effort (lb)	23,700
Overall Length	59ft 3in

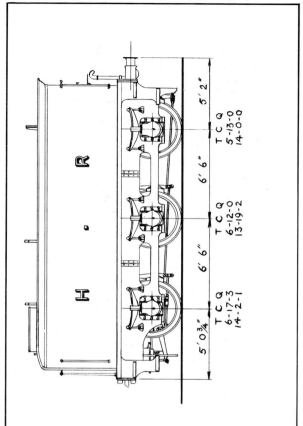

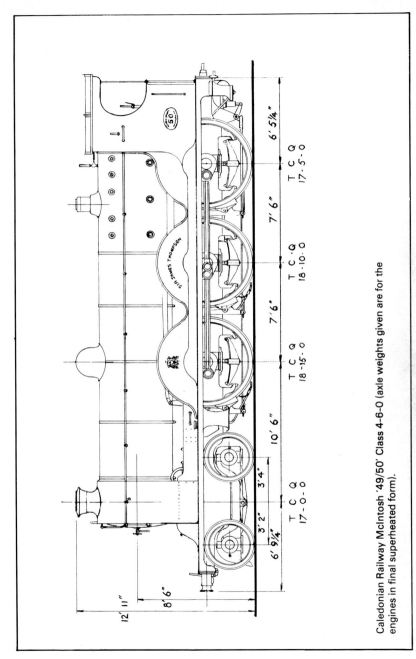

Caledonian Railway McIntosh '49/50' Class 4-6-0 (axle weights given are for the engines in final superheated form).

McIntosh CR '49' class 4-6-0

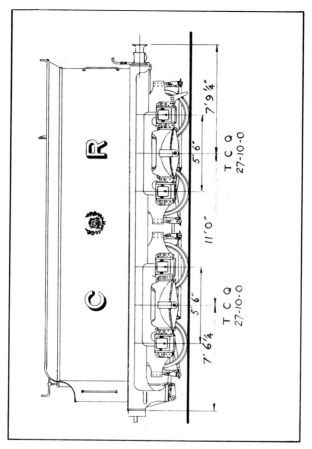

Railway/Class	CR '49' as built	CR '49' superheated
Cylinders (in)	21×26	20¾×26
Driving Wheel Dia	6ft 6in	6ft 6in
Boiler Pressure (lb)	200	175
Max Boiler Dia.	5ft 0in	5ft 0in
Tube Length	17ft 3in	15ft 8in
Tube Heating Surface (sq ft)	2,178	1,509
Firebox	145	145
Total Evaporative	2,323	1,654
Superheater	—	516
Grate Area	26.0	26.0
Adhesion Weight (tons)	53.5	54.5
Engine Weight (tons)	70.0	71.5
Tender Weight (tons)	55.0	55.0
Coal Capacity (tons)	5	5
Water Capacity (galls)	5,000	5,000
Tractive Effort (lb)	25,000	21,300
Overall Length	65ft 6in	65ft 6in

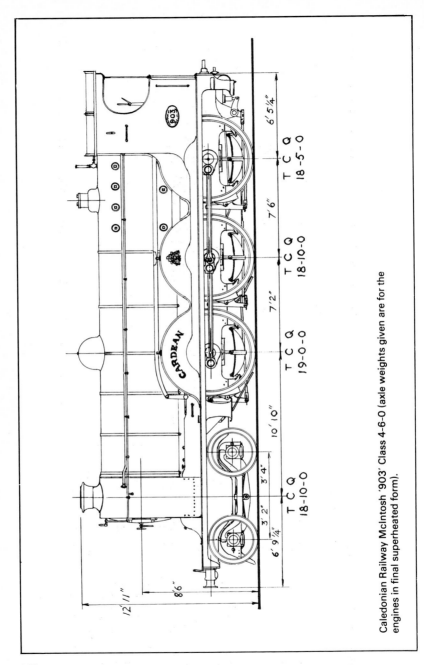

Caledonian Railway McIntosh '903' Class 4-6-0 (axle weights given are for the engines in final superheated form).

McIntosh CR '903' class 4-6-0

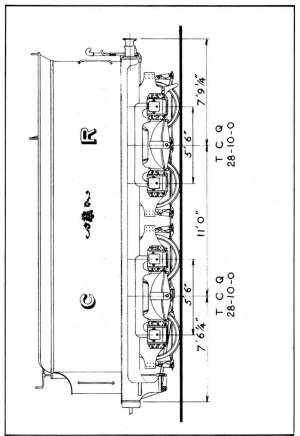

Railway/Class	CR '903' as built	CR '903' superheated
Cylinders (in)	20×26	20¾×26
Driving Wheel Dia.	6ft 6in	6ft 6in
Boiler Pressure (lb)	200	175
Max. Boiler Dia.	5ft 3½in	5ft 3½in
Tube Length	16ft 8in	16ft 8in
Tube Heating Surface (sq ft)	2,118	1,666
Firebox	148	148
Total Evaporative	2,266	1,814
Superheater	—	516
Grate Area	26.0	26.0
Adhesion Weight (tons)	54.5	55.75
Engine Weight (tons)	73.0	74.25
Tender Weight (tons)	57.0	57.0
Coal Capacity (tons)	5	5
Water Capacity (galls)	5,000	5,000
Tractive Effort (lb)	22,700	21,300
Overall Length	65ft 6in	65ft 6in

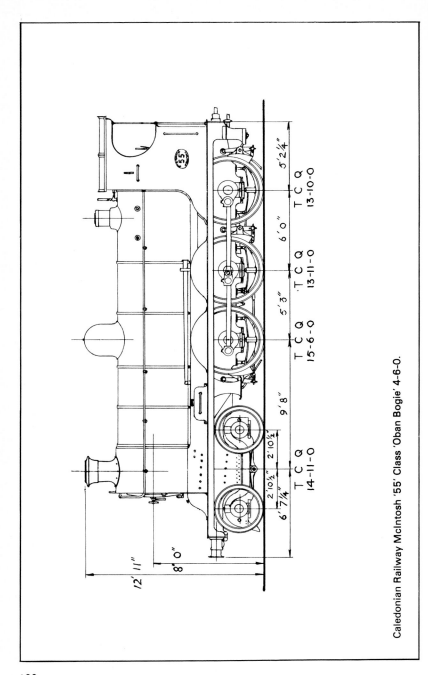

Caledonian Railway McIntosh '55' Class 'Oban Bogie' 4-6-0.

McIntosh 'Oban Bogie' 4-6-0

Railway	CR
Class	'55/51'
Cylinders (in)	19×26
Driving Wheel Dia.	5ft 0in
Boiler Pressure (lb)	175
Max. Boiler Dia.	4ft 9½in
Tube Length	14ft 3½in/13ft 6½in
Tube Heating Surface (sq ft)	1,800/1,705
Firebox	105/105
Total Evaporative	1,905/1,810
Superheater	—
Grate Area	20.6
Adhesion Weight (tons)	42.85
Engine Weight (tons)	57.4*
Tender Weight (tons)	37.3
Coal Capacity (tons)	4½
Water Capacity (galls)	3,000
Tractive Effort (lb)	23,300
Overall Length	54ft 1¼in

* 60 tons after rebuilding with '918' boiler

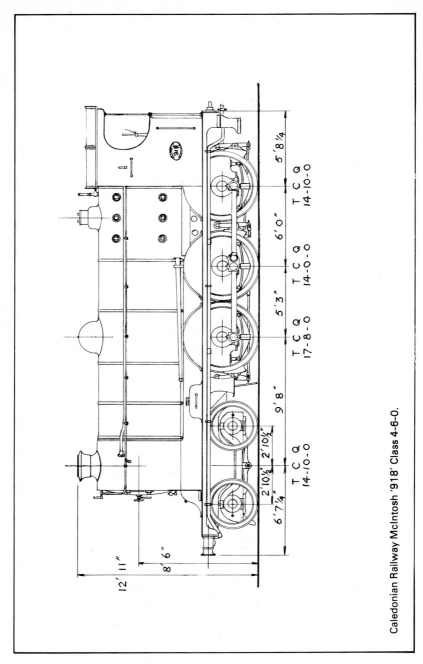

Caledonian Railway McIntosh '918' Class 4-6-0.

McIntosh CR '918', '908', and '179' classes

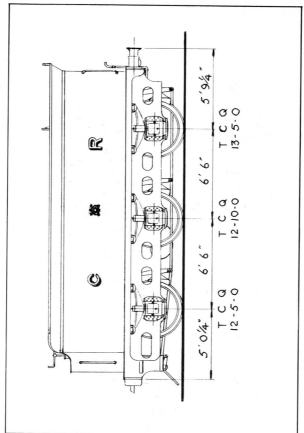

Railway Class	CR '918'	CR '908'	CR '179'
Cylinders (in)	19×26	19×26	19½×26
Driving Wheel Dia	5ft 0in	5ft 9in	5ft 9in
Boiler Pressure (lb)	175	180	170
Max. Boiler Dia.	5ft 3½in	5ft 3½in	5ft 3½in
Tube Length	13ft 6½in	14ft 11$\frac{7}{8}$in	14ft 11$\frac{7}{8}$in
Tube Heating Surface (sq ft)	1,716	1,895	1,439
Firebox	128	128	128
Total Evaporative	1,844	2,023	1,567
Superheater	—	—	403
Grate Area	21.0	21.0	21.0
Adhesion Wt (tons)	45.9	49.0	51.25
Engine Wt (tons)	60.4	64.0	68.5
Tender Wt (tons)	38.0	38.0	38.0
Coal Capacity (tons)	4½	4½	4½
Water Cap.(gal)	3,570	3,570	3,570
Tractive Effort (lb)	23,300	20,800	20,700
Overall Length	57ft 6in	58ft 11in	59ft 6in

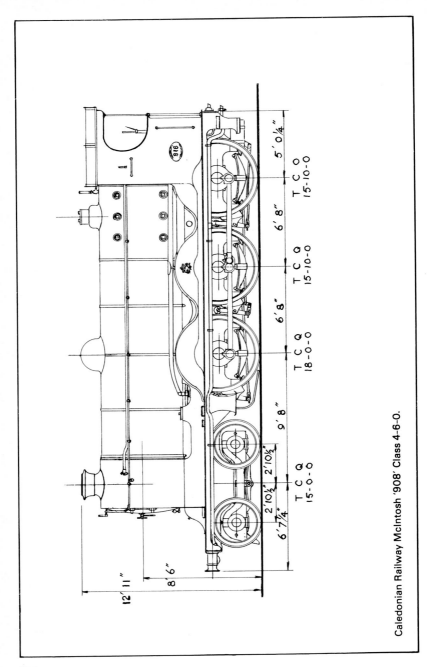

Caledonian Railway McIntosh '908' Class 4-6-0.

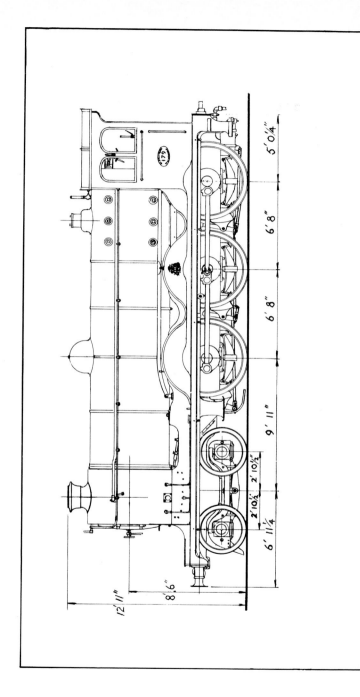

Caledonian Railway McIntosh '179' Class 4-6-0.

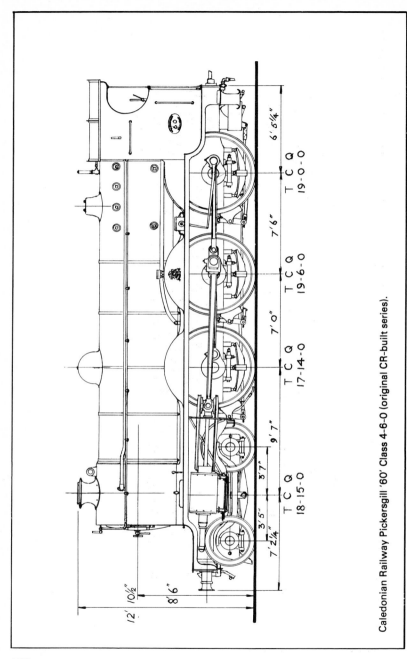

Caledonian Railway Pickersgill '60' Class 4-6-0 (original CR-built series).

Pickersgill CR '60' class 4-6-0

Railway	CR batch	LMS batch
Class	'60'	'60'
Cylinders (in)	20×26	20½×26
Driving Wheel Dia.	6ft 1in	6ft 1in
Boiler Pressure (lb)	175	180
Max Boiler Dia.	5ft 3½in	5ft 3½in
Tube Length	15ft 3in	15ft 3in
Tube Heating Surface (sq ft)	1,529	1,529
Firebox	147	147
Total Evaporative	1,676	1,676
Superheater	258	258
Grate Area	25.5	25.5
Adhesion Weight (tons)	56.5	56.0
Engine Weight (tons)	75.0	74.75
Tender Weight (tons)	46.5	41.5*
Coal Capacity (tons)	6	5
Water Capacity (gals)	4,200	3,500
Tractive Effort (lb)	21,200	22,900
Overall Length	62ft 6in	62ft 6in

* 43.9 tons with water pick up fitted.

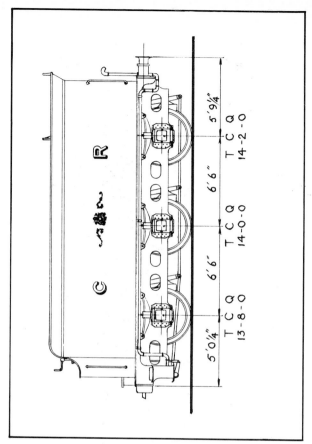

5'0¼" 6'6" 6'6" 5'9¼"

T C Q T C Q T C Q T C Q
13 - 8 - 0 14 - 0 - 0 14 - 2 - 0

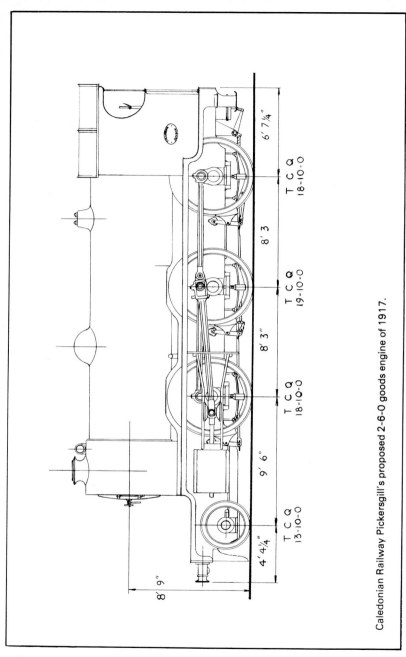

Caledonian Railway Pickersgill's proposed 2-6-0 goods engine of 1917.

Proposed Pickersgill CR Goods 2-6-0, 1917

Railway	CR
Class	
Cylinders (in)	21×28
Driving Wheel Dia	5ft 8in
Boiler Pressure (lb)	175
Max Boiler Dia.	5ft 7¼in
Tube Length	13ft 3in
Tube heating Surface (sq ft)	1,670
Firebox	165
Total Evaporative	1,835
Superheater	165
Grate Area	27.5
Adhesion Weight (tons)	56.5
Engine Weight (tons)	70.0
Tractive Effort (lb)	27,000

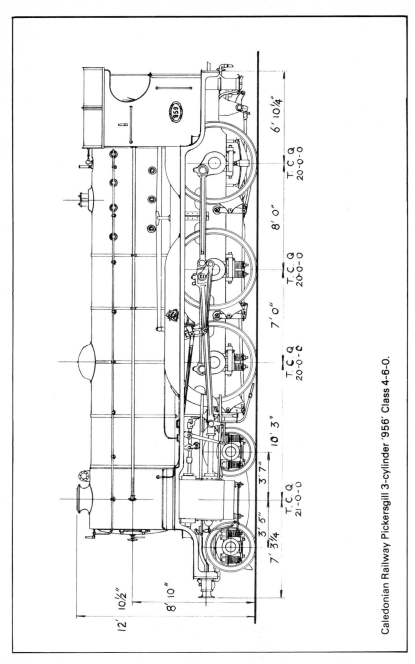

Caledonian Railway Pickersgill 3-cylinder '956' Class 4-6-0.

Pickersgill 3-cylinder CR '956' class 4-6-0

Railway	*CR*
Class	*'956'*
Cylinders (in)	(3) 18½×26
Driving Wheel Dia	6ft 1in
Boiler Pressure (lb)	180
Max Boiler Dia	5ft 9in
Tube Length	16ft 0in
Tube Heating Surface (sq ft)	2,200
Firebox	170
Total Evaporative	2,370
Superheater	270
Grate Area	28.0
Adhesion Weight (tons)	60.0
Engine Weight (tons)	81.0
Tender Weight (tons)	48.0
Coal Capacity (tons)	5½
Water Capacity (gals)	4,500
Tractive Effort (lb)	28,000
Overall Length	63ft 8in

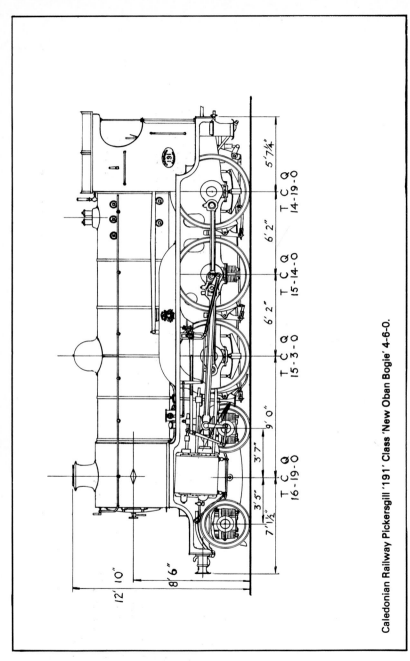

Caledonian Railway Pickersgill '191' Class 'New Oban Bogie' 4-6-0.

Pickersgill CR '191' class 'New Oban Bogie'
4-6-0

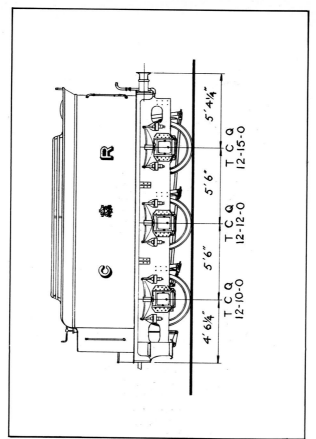

Railway	CR
Class	'191'
Cylinders (in)	19½x26
Driving Wheel Dia	5ft 6in
Boiler Pressure (lb)	185
Max. Boiler Dia	4ft 9¼in
Tube Length	13ft 6in
Tube heating Surface (sq ft)	1,707
Firebox	116
Total Evaporative	1,823
Superheater	—
Grate Area	21.9
Adhesion Weight (tons)	45.8
Engine Weight (tons)	62.75
Tender Weight (tons)	37.85
Coal Capacity (tons)	4½
Water Capacity (gals)	3,000
Tractive Effort (lb)	23,600
Overall Length	55ft 5in

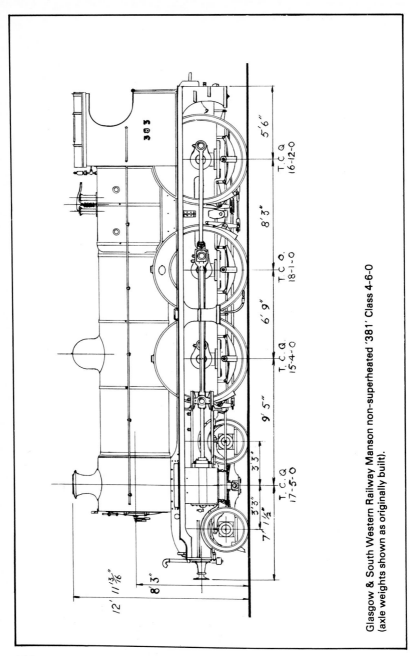

Glasgow & South Western Railway Manson non-superheated '381' Class 4-6-0 (axle weights shown as originally built).

Manson G&SWR Non-superheated 4-6-0

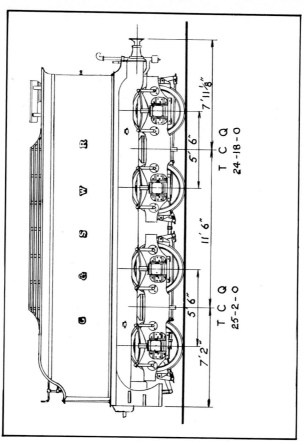

Railway/Class	G&SWR '381'	511 rebuilt 1920
Cylinders (in)	20x26	20x26
Driving Wheel Dia	6ft 6in	6ft 6in
Boiler Pressure (lb)	180	175
Max. Boiler Dia.	4ft 9¼in	4ft 9¼in
Tube Length	15ft 8⅛in	15ft 8⅛in
Tube Heating Surface (sq ft)	1,721	1,721
Firebox	131	140
Total Evaporative	1,852	1,861
Superheater	—	—
Grate Area	24.5	27.0
Adhesion Wt (tons)	49.85/51.1	51.75
Engine Wt (tons)	67.1	67.95
Tender Wt (tons)	50.3	44.0 (50 8-wheel tender)
Coal Capacity (tons)	4	4
Water Capacity (gals)	4,100	4,100
Tractive Effort (lb)	20,400	19,900
Overall Length	64ft 6in	

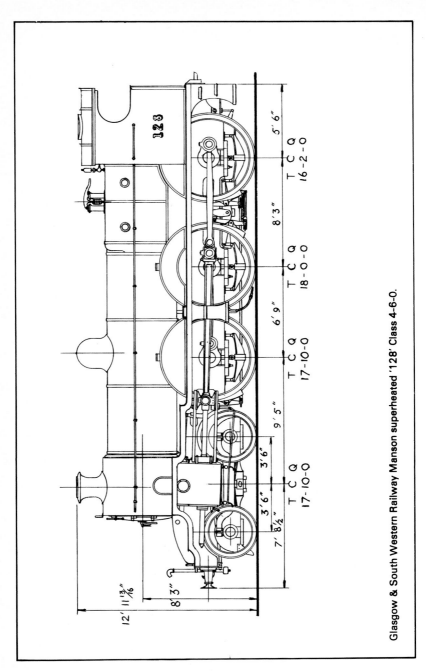

Glasgow & South Western Railway Manson superheated '128' Class 4-6-0.

Manson G&SWR Superheated 4-6-0

Railway/Class	G&SWR 128/129*
Cylinders (in)	21×26
Driving Wheel Dia.	6ft 6in
Boiler Pressure (lb)	160(165)
Max. Boiler Dia.	4ft 9¼in
Tube Length	15ft 8⅛in
Tube Heating Surface (sq ft)	1,430
Firebox	130
Total Evaporative	1,560
Superheater	445
Grate Area	24.5
Adhesion, Weight (tons)	53.0/52.7*
Engine Weight (tons)	69.1/71.35*
Tender Weight (tons)	50.05
Coal Capacity (tons)	4
Water Capacity (gals)	4100
Tractive Effort (lb)	20,000
Overall Length	65ft 1in

*fitted with Weir feedwater heater.

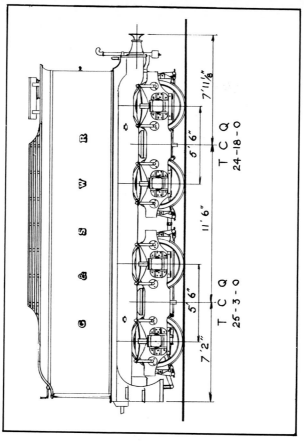

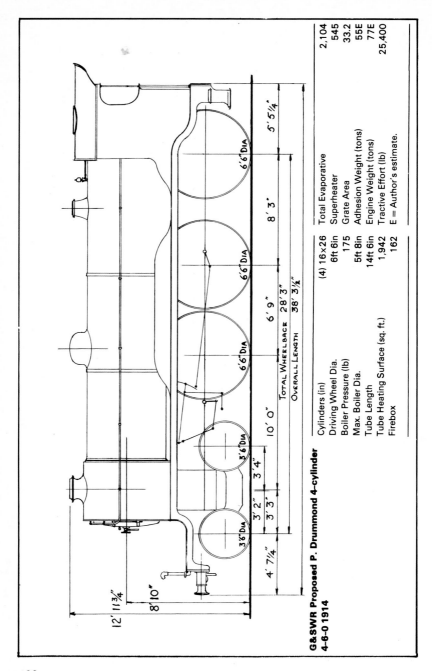

G&SWR Proposed P. Drummond 4-cylinder 4–6–0 1914

Cylinders (in)	(4) 16×26
Driving Wheel Dia.	6ft 6in
Boiler Pressure (lb)	175
Max. Boiler Dia.	5ft 8in
Tube Length	14ft 6in
Tube Heating Surface (sq. ft.)	1,942
Firebox	162
Total Evaporative	2,104
Superheater	545
Grate Area	33.2
Adhesion Weight (tons)	55E
Engine Weight (tons)	77E
Tractive Effort (lb)	25,400
E = Author's estimate.	

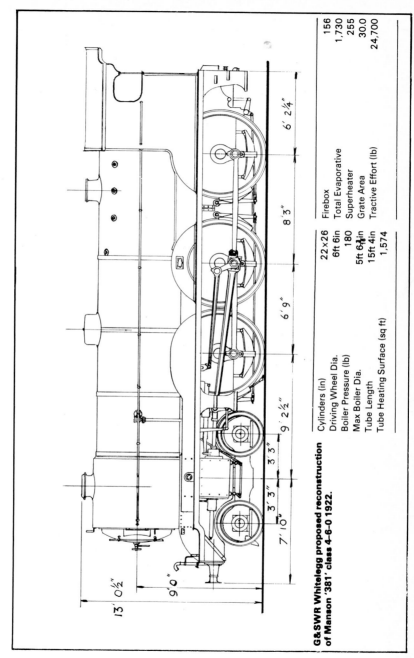

G&SWR Whitelegg proposed reconstruction of Manson '381' class 4-6-0 1922.

Cylinders (in)	22x26	Firebox	156
Driving Wheel Dia.	6ft 6in	Total Evaporative	1,730
Boiler Pressure (lb)	180	Superheater	255
Max Boiler Dia.	5ft 6¼in	Grate Area	30.0
Tube Length	15ft 4in	Tractive Effort (lb)	24,700
Tube Heating Surface (sq ft)	1,574		

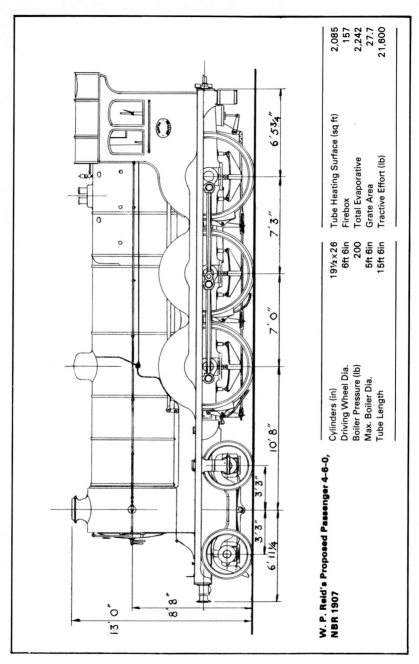

**W. P. Reid's Proposed Passenger 4-6-0,
NBR 1907**

Cylinders (in)	19¼ × 26	Tube Heating Surface (sq ft)	2,085
Driving Wheel Dia.	6ft 6in	Firebox	157
Boiler Pressure (lb)	200	Total Evaporative	2,242
Max. Boiler Dia.	5ft 6in	Grate Area	27.7
Tube Length	15ft 6in	Tractive Effort (lb)	21,600

122

Bibliography

E. S. Cox, *Locomotive Panorama Vol 1*, Ian Allan 1965.

E. S. Cox, *Locomotive Panorama Vol 2*, Ian Allan 1966.

E. S. Cox, *Chronicles of Steam*, Ian Allan 1967.

J. A. B. Hamilton, *Britain's Railways in World War I*, George Allen & Unwin 1967.

Campbell Highet, *Scottish Locomotive History 1831-1923*, George Allen & Unwin 1971.

H. Holcroft, *Locomotive Adventure*, Ian Allan 1962.

A. B. MacLeod, *The McIntosh Locomotives of the Caledonian Railway*, Ian Allan 1944.

O. S. Nock, *The Caledonian Railway*, Ian Allan 1962.

O. S. Nock, *The Highland Railway*, Ian Allan 1965.

David L. Smith, *Tales of the Glasgow & South Western Railway*, Ian Allan 1961.

John Thomas, *The Callander & Oban Railway*, David & Charles 1966.

John Thomas, *Gretna, Britain's Worst Railway Disaster (1915)* David & Charles 1969.

John Thomas, *The North British Atlantics*, David & Charles 1972.

The Glasgow and South Western Railway 1850-1923, published by the Stephenson Locomotive Society 1950.

The Highland Railway Company and its Constituents and Successors 1855-1955 published by the Stephenson Locomotive Society 1955.

The Report of the Bridge Stress Committee, HMSO 1928.

Various issues of:

Bulletin of the International Railway Congress (English edition), *Cassier's Magazine, The Engineer, Engineering, Journal of the Stephenson Locomotive Society, The Locomotive, Railway Carriage & Wagon Review, The Railway Engineer, The Railway Magazine, Railway World, Trains Illustrated.*